Masters: Beadweaving

VALERIE HECTOR ■ SHARON M. DONOVAN
DIANE FITZGERALD ■ LAURA WILLITS
ANN TEVEPAUGH MITCHELL ■ MARCIA DECOSTER
JOYCE J. SCOTT ■ JEANETTE AHLGREN
NATASHA ST. MICHAEL ■ AMOLIA WILLOWSONG
LINDA FIFIELD ■ NANC MEINHARDT ■ SONYA CLARK
DAVID K. CHATT ■ RACHEL NELSON-SMITH
MAGGIE MEISTER ■ SHARMINI WIRASEKARA
LAURA LEONARD ■ LESLIE FRAZIER ■ DON PIERCE

LAURA MCCABE ■ MADELYN C. RICKS

MELANIE POTTER ■ HUIB PETERSEN

SHERRY SERAFINI ■ WENDY ELLSWORTH

CYNTHIA RUTLEDGE ■ REBECCA BROWN-THOMPSON

SUSAN ETCOFF FRAERMAN ■ ELEANOR LUX

KAREN PAUST ■ MARCIE STONE

DALLAS LOVETT ■ MARGO C. FIELD

VIRGINIA L. BLAKELOCK ■ JO ANN BAUMANN

Masters: Beadweaving

Major Works by Leading Artists

Curated by Carol Wilcox Wells

LARK BOOKS

A Division of Sterling Publishing Co., Inc.
New York / London

SENIOR EDITOR
Ray Hemachandra

EDITOR
Julie Hale

ART DIRECTOR
Dana Irwin

ART PRODUCTION
Jeff Hamilton

COVER DESIGNER
Cindy LaBreacht

FRONT COVER, LEFT TO RIGHT
Diane Fitzgerald
Collage Necklace III, 1998
Photo by artist

Susan Etcoff Fraerman
Hecuba, 1996
Photo by Tom Van Eynde

Amolia Willowsong
Willow's Song, 2007
Photo by Tim Barnwell

NanC Meinhardt
Fable Vessel, 1993
Photo by Tom Van Eynde

Marcia DeCoster
Urchin Lariat, 2007
Photo by artist

BACK COVER, LEFT TO RIGHT
Linda Fifield
Earth and Fire #71, 2001
Photo by Jack T. Fifield

Ann Tevepaugh Mitchell
Kosovo, 2002
Photo by Dean Powell

Natasha St. Michael
Thriving, 2007
Photo by Paul Litherland

SPINE
Sonya Clark
Holding Hands, 2005
Photo by Tom McInvaille

Library of Congress Cataloging-in-Publication Data

Masters : beadweaving : major works by leading artists / curated by Carol Wilcox Wells ; editor, Ray Hemachandra. -- 1st ed.
    p. cm.
  Includes index.
  ISBN-13: 978-1-60059-039-9 (pb-with flaps : alk. paper)
  1. Beadwork. 2. Beads. I. Wells, Carol Wilcox, 1949- II. Hemachandra, Ray. III. Title.
  NK3650.M36 2008
  746.5--dc22

                          2008001485

10 9 8 7 6 5 4 3 2 1

First Edition

Published by Lark Books, A Division of
Sterling Publishing Co., Inc.
387 Park Avenue South, New York, NY 10016

Text © 2008, Lark Books

Photography © 2008, Artist/Photographer as specified

Distributed in Canada by Sterling Publishing,
c/o Canadian Manda Group, 165 Dufferin Street
Toronto, Ontario, Canada M6K 3H6

Distributed in the United Kingdom by GMC Distribution Services,
Castle Place, 166 High Street, Lewes, East Sussex, England BN7 1XU

Distributed in Australia by Capricorn Link (Australia) Pty Ltd.,
P.O. Box 704, Windsor, NSW 2756 Australia

If you have questions or comments about this book, please contact:
Lark Books
67 Broadway
Asheville, NC 28801
828-253-0467

Manufactured in China

ISBN 13: 978-1-60059-039-9

For information about custom editions, special sales, and premium and corporate purchases, please contact the Sterling Special Sales Department at 800-805-5489 or specialsales@sterlingpub.com.

Contents

Introduction

What is it about beads that captures the hearts and souls of so many talented artists? What seduces them to turn away from other artistic mediums and embrace beadweaving? The work is time-consuming and tedious. It's solitary. And yet it's undeniably addictive.

Many artists are captivated by how light interacts with the beads. The tactile act of forming a beaded fabric or piece of wearable art is challenging and inspiring. The meditative quality of working with beads enthralls, too. The beads force people to slow down in a world full of constant demands.

In fact, for some artists, *all* these things draw them to this clean, portable medium of artistic expression. Whether the beadweaver works intuitively in the moment, like Ann Tevepaugh Mitchell creating sculptures with improvisational creativity, or from a preconceived plan, like Jeanette Ahlgren executing her fantastic, minutely detailed wire-woven vessels, the undertaking fulfills the expressive needs for creativity and craftsmanship. Passion moves through the mind, eyes, and heart straight into the hands, flowing seamlessly out into the world to bring joy to both the maker and the receiver.

Looking at all the master artists included in this book—and just skimming the surface, really, of the incredible diversity of talent represented in today's beadweaving community—the differences in styles are pronounced, but the base influences on the works are consistent. The major inspirations fall into simple, repeating categories: the natural world; narrative and social issues; historical references; color and design; and life experiences. Within these groupings, each of these influential artists and teachers makes her or his distinctive contribution to beadweaving's reach, range, and depth. Compare the similarly titled *Sunset and Sapphire* (page 248) by Karen Paust with *Mango Salsa Sunset* (page 82) by Amolia Willowsong. These sharply different pieces reflect wonderful extremes of realism and impressionism, yet both artists capture a particular moment and portray it with their particular artistic vision.

Many artists use multiple techniques in each piece, taking advantage of the different capabilities inherent in each stitch. When I wrote *Creative Bead Weaving* for Lark Books in 1996, even most of the world's leading beadweavers used just one stitch per project, and so I wrote a chapter about combining stitches. It's heartening to see the growth in this regard. Judging by all the work I reviewed for this book, peyote stitch is still the most popular technique, because of its ease of use and versatility. Right-angle weave is next in popularity, and other stitches and techniques showcased in this volume include herringbone, netting, fringing, brick, square, spiral rope, wire weaving, ladder stitch, chevron chain, African helix, polygon weave, Chinese hexagonal pillow, and triangle weave. Many of these stitches are used in combination with others, and loom work and embroidery are also part of the mix.

Peyote stitch produces a vertical brick pattern, meaning that straight vertical lines can be made but not straight horizontal lines. Peyote's variations include flat, odd and even count, and tubular. It can be increased and decreased along the outside edges and within. The bead count per stitch can be changed, and it can be ruffled and spiked. A change in tension can produce a supple fabric or beads that stand at attention. Comparison is useful: Joyce J. Scott (page 56) and Madelyn C. Ricks (page 176) work with peyote stitch to achieve completely different effects. Scott utilizes the freeform and dimensional aspects of peyote, while Ricks works in a highly controlled environment creating detailed patterns. Despite the dramatic dichotomy between their approaches, the two artists each use peyote stitch to great advantage.

I like to ponder the spirit of the beadweavers' intent as I examine their unique styles, and I invite you to do the same. The artists themselves offer insight in their brief commentaries that accompany the pieces. Each work presented here enriches the arc of beadweaving's history and extends the promise of the medium into the future. All the pieces are distinguished by grand artistic inspiration, fine technical expertise, and the impassioned, relentless commitment of their makers. Selecting these works has been my job and my joy. Your task—and I trust your pleasure, as well—is to experience for yourself the exquisite and diverse masterworks of three dozen of the very best beadweavers working today.

— Carol Wilcox Wells

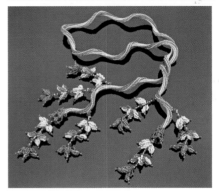

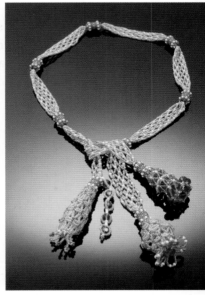

Beadwork by Carol Wilcox Wells, clockwise from top left: **Infinities Loop Necklace** (2007); **Sea Pods** (2007); **Trillium Spiral** (2007); **Dazzling Dahlia Brooch** (2005)

Valerie Hector

COMBINING BEADWEAVING and silversmithing techniques, Valerie Hector has launched to the forefront of American bead artistry. Her work marries historical inspiration with contemporary flare. Whether utilizing peyote stitch, right-angle weave, or various Chinese beading techniques, Hector's pieces emphasize the value of partnering form and function. Her fantastic clasps, for example, are integral parts of the pieces, seamlessly reflecting the other design elements. Hector heightens viewer interest through her use of architecturally organic shapes and bright, clear colors. When she introduces a pattern in the beadwork, it typically involves highly contrasted hues. Many pieces also are loaded with texture—see the points and layering of the divine *Rust Lotus Necklace*. Hector approaches her work as a quintessential craftsperson: She owns every aspect of her pieces, and they all are brilliantly conceived and executed.

▲ **Rust Lotus Necklace** | 2003
2¾ x 12½ x 4¾ inches (7 x 31.8 x 12.1 cm)
Synthetic resin beads, sterling silver
beads; cubic right-angle weave
Photo by Larry Sanders

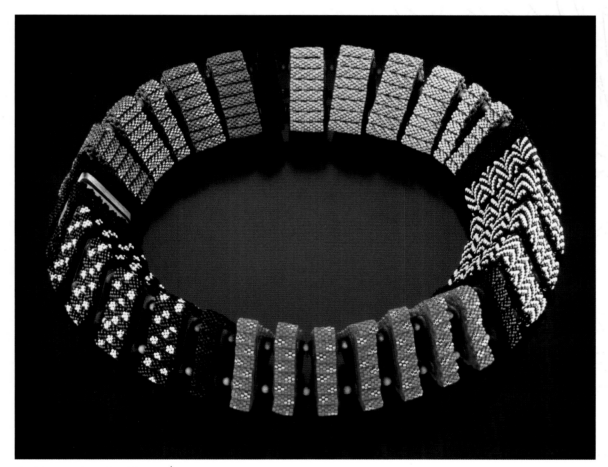

▲ **Proxemics Necklace** | 2004

1½ x 9½ x 2½ inches (3.8 x 24.1 x 6.4 cm)

Glass beads, sterling silver beads, sterling silver
spacers, sterling silver clasp; peyote stitch

Photo by Larry Sanders

▲ **Sterling Accordion Bracelet** | 2006

1¾ x 3¾ x ¾ inches (4.4 x 9.5 x 1.9 cm)
Sterling silver beads, sterling silver clasp;
cubic right-angle weave

Photo by Larry Sanders

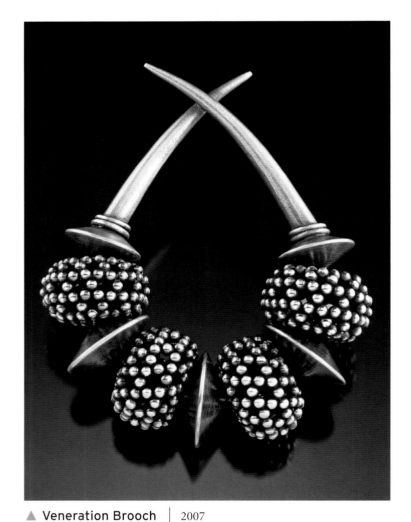

▲ **Veneration Brooch** | 2007

4⅞ x 3¾ x 1¼ inches (12.4 x 9.5 x 3.2 cm)
Sterling silver beads, sterling silver armature;
Chinese hexagonal pillows technique

Photo by Larry Sanders

" It's a constant struggle to balance color and form in a single piece. If I were forced to choose, I would give up color and concentrate on form. Form is not more elemental than color, but somehow it feels that way to me, as if form, done well, can be essence. "

▲ **Lotus Necklace** | 2006
¾ x 11 x 1¾ inches (1.9 x 27.9 x 4.4 cm)
Sterling silver beads, sterling silver
clasp; cubic right-angle weave
Photo by Larry Sanders

Confetti Bracelet | 2000 ▶

1 x 3½ x ⅜ inches (2.5 x 8.9 x 1 cm)
Glass beads, metal beads, sterling
silver armature; peyote stitch
Photo by Hap Sakwa

" One of the most exciting
aspects about beadwork
is that it's infinite—we
will never be able to
learn as much as there is
to know about the past
of this medium, not to
mention its present. And
we will never be able to
make all the pieces we'd
like to make, learn all the
techniques there are to
know, or obtain all the
beads we'd like to have. **"**

◀ **Confetti Necklace** | 2000

⅜ x 18 x 1 inches (1 x 45.7 x 2.5 cm)
Glass beads, metal beads, sterling
silver armatures, 14-karat gold links
and clasp; peyote stitch
Photo by Hap Sakwa

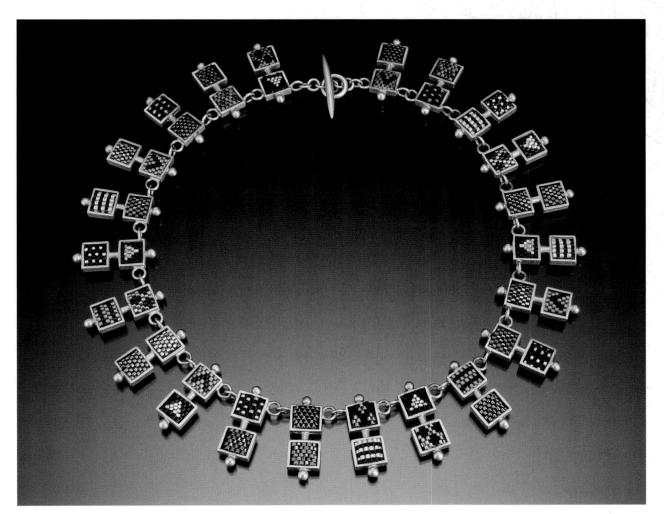

▲ **Confetti Reversible Necklace** | 2000

⅜ x 20 x 1 inches (1 x 50.8 x 2.5 cm)
Glass beads, metal beads,
14-karat gold; peyote stitch

Photo by Hap Sakwa

Celestial Spheres Necklace | 2004 ►

1½ x 22 inches (3.8 x 55.8 cm)
Glass beads, sterling silver beads, synthetic resin beads, cinnabar beads, sterling silver clasp; cubic right-angle weave, various Chinese bead polyhedron techniques

Photo by Larry Sanders

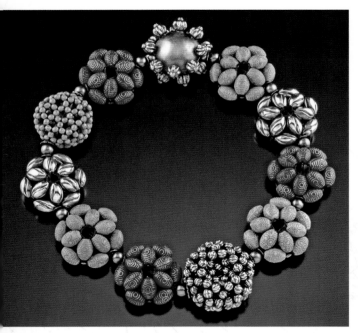

▲ **China Spring Necklace** | 2006

11½ x ¾ inches (29.2 x 1.9 cm)
Glass beads, sterling silver beads, sterling silver clasp; various Chinese netting techniques

Photo by Larry Sanders

▲ **Red Star Brooch** | 2002

½ x 3¾ x 3¾ inches (1.3 x 9.5 x 9.5 cm)
Seed beads, metal beads, sterling silver
armature; peyote stitch

Photo by Larry Sanders

*" I'm convinced that some of
the most original beadworking
techniques in the world were
invented by mistake. Someone
made a wrong stitch or added
too many or too few beads
someplace. A few of my more
promising designs began in
just this way. Or, small pieces
of beadwork and metal came
together on my desk quite by
accident. I like when things
happen at random like this,
as if they were sent by the
universe or some kindly
beadwork ancestor. "*

Sharon M. Donovan

THE RESPONSE I HAVE NOW to the work of Sharon M. Donovan is the same as the first time I saw it: I'm blown away. Her ideas are simple and strong, and they take shape as glorious combinations of bead, thread, and metal. First, Donovan fabricates metal into geometric shapes—some flat, some three-dimensional— and then she flows her beadweaving within those shapes and lines. In *Stone Weave I*, the onyx, hematite, and sterling silver beads are blended to enhance a central stone. The "V" shape of the weaving carries the design a step further, and the texture of the beads are juxtaposed purposefully against the smoothness of the stone. The overall effect is perfect. Donovan sometimes uses her beads to create dimensional form, as in *Beaded Pods I, II, & III*; the beads are integral parts of the overall structure of the work. For the most part, bead colors are muted in Donovan's weaving, and so they do not present distractions to the pieces' fine quality and elegance.

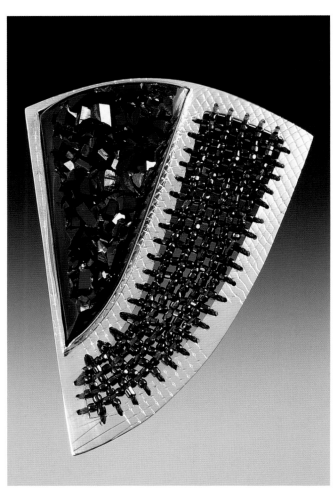

Blue Drusy Brooch II | 1993 ▶

2 x 4 x ½ inches (5.1 x 10.2 x 1.3 cm)
Triple-cut iridescent Czech glass beads,
drusy quartz with titanium, sterling
silver frame; fabricated, woven

Photo by Larry Sanders

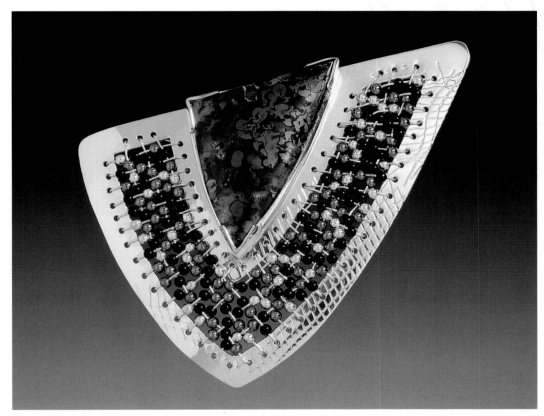

▲ **Stone Weave I** | 1996

2 x 4 x ½ inches (5.1 x 10.2 x 1.3 cm)
Psilomolane beads, sterling silver
beads, onyx beads, hematite beads,
sterling silver wire; fabricated, woven

Photo by Larry Sanders

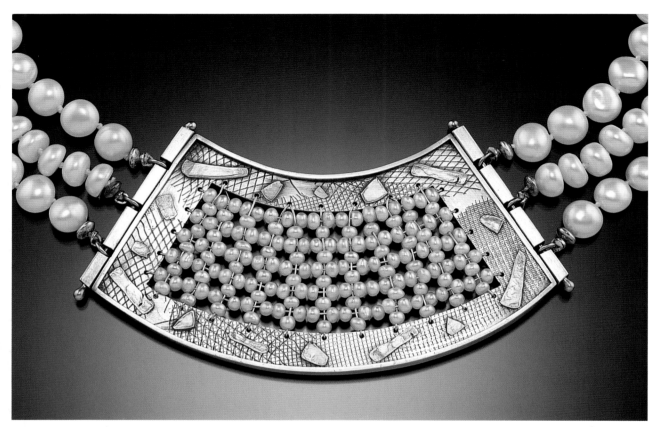

▲ **White Pearl Fandango I** | 2002

2 x 24 x ¼ inches (5.1 x 61 x 0.6 cm)
Freshwater pearls, sterling silver frame,
14-karat gold, patina, gold wire;
fabricated, woven

Photo by Larry Sanders

" I've always been fascinated by jewelry. One
of my earliest memories is playing with my
mother's earrings, much to her annoyance,
while she was wearing them. "

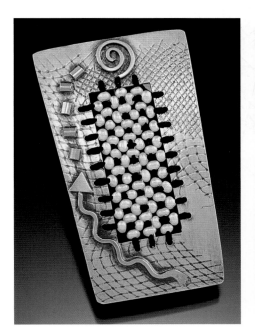

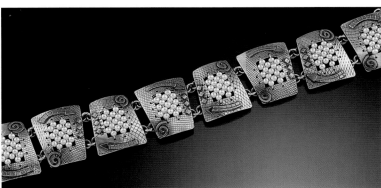

Wonky Brooch | 2007

1 x 2 inches (2.5 x 5.1 cm)
Freshwater pearls, sterling silver
frame, 14-karat gold, patina,
silk thread; fabricated, woven

Photo by Larry Sanders

Wonky Earrings | 2007

1 x 1¼ inches
(2.5 x 3.2 cm) each
Freshwater pearls,
sterling silver frame,
14-karat gold, silk thread,
patina; fabricated, woven

Photo by Larry Sanders

Wonky Bracelet II | 2007

1 x 7½ inches (2.5 x 19.1 cm)
Freshwater pearls, sterling silver
frame, 14-karat gold, patina, gold
wire; fabricated, woven

Photo by Larry Sanders

SHARON M. **DONOVAN**

" I firmly believed I could not be an artist. I also believed I had to try anyway. My first jewelry-making materials and tools were seed beads, a small loom, and, unfortunately, cotton thread. My loom pieces usually fell apart before I could finish them. I still tug too hard on thread. But, now, I use better thread. "

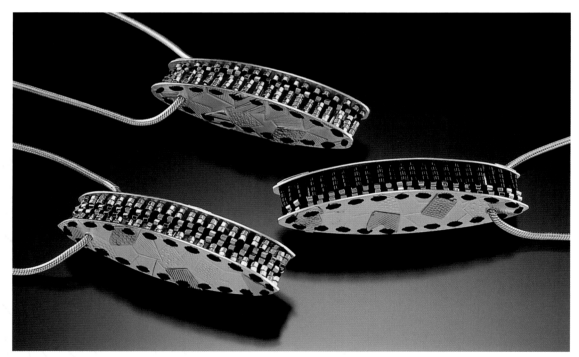

▲ **Beaded Pods I, II, & III** | 2003

2 x 1 x ½ inches (5.1 x 2.5 x 1.3 cm)
Cylinder seed beads, sterling silver
frame, 14-karat gold, silk thread;
fabricated, woven

Photo by Larry Sanders

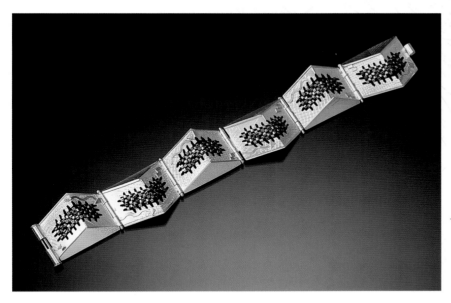

◀ **2.5D Bracelet** │ 2001

1 x 7½ x ½ inches (2.5 x 19.1 x 1.3 cm)
Seed beads, 14-karat gold, silk thread,
sterling silver frame; fabricated, woven

Photo by Larry Sanders

Martian Handcuff │ 2004 ▶

3 x 4¾ x ½ inches (7.6 x 12.1 x 1.3 cm)
Cylinder seed beads, 14-karat gold,
sterling silver frame, silk thread;
fabricated, woven

Photo by Larry Sanders

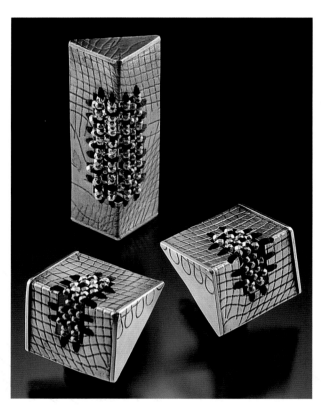

◀ **Box Set** | 2007

Earrings, ¾ x ½ x ½ (1.9 x 1.3 x 1.3 cm)
Aluminum Victorian beads, metal beads, silk
thread, sterling silver frame; fabricated, woven

Photo by Larry Sanders

The Box | 1995 ▶

2 x 4 x 3 inches (5.1 x 10.2 x 7.6 cm)
Triple-cut iridescent Czech glass
beads, silk thread, sterling silver
frame; fabricated, woven

Photo by Larry Sanders

▲ **Drusy Chrysacolla** │ 2006

    2 x 4 x ½ inches (5.1 x 10.2 x 1.3 cm)
    Glass beads, drusy chrysacolla, sterling silver frame,
    14-karat gold, gold wire; fabricated, woven

    Photo by Larry Sanders

▲ **Blue Drusy Earrings** │ 2000

    1 x 3 x ½ inches (2.5 x 7.6 x 1.3 cm)
    Triple-cut iridescent Czech glass beads,
    drusy quartz with titanium, silk thread,
    sterling silver frame; fabricated, woven

    Photo by Larry Sanders

" The way I describe the positive parts of my job is this: I go to interesting cities. I meet wonderful

people with whom I have a lot in common. They stand around and tell me how nice my work is, and

some of them give me money. I'm grateful for the blessings my work brings to me. I get to spend part

of each day doing what I love. **"**

————————

Diane Fitzgerald

FLORAL AND ABSTRACT PATTERNING reach glorious heights in Diane Fitzgerald's work. Organic shapes flow with graduated color, and linear shapes burst with primary contrasts. The relaxed sense of whimsy and letting go in *Pod People* can be juxtaposed with the tight control evidenced in *Flowering Pyramid*, keeping viewers on their visual toes. The simplicity of black-and-white design in *Amazon Collar* presents a sharp and striking contrast to the overall presentation of the piece amidst bold colors. Fitzgerald's thoughtful explorations are unpredictable but always executed with ingenuity and precision. In the leaf shapes of *Ginkgo Leaf Necklace I*, each ruffled fan stands alone yet also combines with its nearby neighbors to create a gorgeous effect. Playing with her beads—beadweaving just because it's fun—is what makes Fitzgerald happy, and her passion is always revealed in her engaging, outstanding work.

Pod People | 1999 ▶
3 inches (7.6 cm) tall
Seed beads, metal
beads; Zulu rib stitch
Photo by artist

◀ **Ginkgo Leaf Necklace I** │ 1995

36 inches (91.4 cm) long
Cylinder beads, seed beads, Nymo thread;
brick stitch, peyote stitch, square stitch

Photo by artist

" It was a dark and stormy night, and someone was knocking on my door. A young woman I'd chanced upon was there, wearing a simple rope-like necklace made of tiny beads. When I admired it, she offered to show me how to do something called 'peyote stitch.' Within minutes I was hooked on beadweaving. "

Sea Anemone Garden | 1994 ▶

½ x 1 x 8 inches (1.3 x 2.5 x 20.3 cm)
Seed beads, Nymo thread, leather,
snap; loom woven

Photo by artist

DIANE FITZGERALD

▼ **Amazon Collar** │ 2005

18 x 15 inches (45.7 x 38.1 cm)
Cylinder beads, feathers, bone
spacers, cord, felt; brick stitch

Photo by artist

▲ **Paisley Necklace** │ 2000

10 x 8 x ¼ inches (25.4 x 20.3 x 0.6 cm)
Cylinder beads, seed beads, three-cut
beads, Nymo thread; brick stitch

Photo by artist

" The myriad ways in which beads can be assembled with a thread and needle constantly amaze me. Each stitch offers something unique to be considered when designing a new piece, so I consider which stitch will provide the texture and arrangement of beads that are right for my vision. For this reason, I encourage beaders to be as fluent in as many stitches as possible. "

▲ **Flowering Pyramid** | 2006

6 x 6 x 6 inches (15.2 x 15.2 x 15.2 cm)
Cylinder beads, metal beads, chain;
peyote stitch

Photos by artist

◀ **Untitled** | 1999

10 x 8 inches (25.4 x 20.3 cm)
Cylinder beads, seed beads,
other beads, metal disk; brick
stitch, figure-eight chain

Photos by artist

FITZGERALD

DIANE

◀ **Collage Necklace III** │ 1998
7 x 11 inches (17.8 x 27.9 cm)
Cylinder beads, seed beads,
other beads, Nymo thread, pearls,
metal leaves; freeform netting
Photo by artist

" My self-expression in
beadwork springs from a love
of color and design. My work
isn't political or whimsical.
No deep soul-searching or
inner turmoil is struggling to
be expressed in what I create.
I strive only to create
something beautiful that
gives me, and hopefully
others, pleasure. "

◄ **Personal Symbols Necklace** │ 2005

1 x 24 inches (2.5 x 61 cm)

Cylinder beads, nylon thread; brick stitch

Photo by artist

DIANE FITZGERALD

Laura Willits

LANDSCAPES BOTH RURAL and urban, filled with shadows and light, are recurrent motifs in Laura Willits' work. She brings viewers to the times of day when mystery informs their surroundings, and she dazzles the eye. Twilight is the signature moment of Willits' loom-woven paintings. Her stellar compositions create visual movement and link viewers to the stories being told and implied. The scenes are familiar and feel almost iconic. *A Maze* and *Arches Gap*—see the close-up detail photographs of these pieces—begin to suggest the complexity of all Willits' work. Her choosing of bead colors to create subtle shadings is a monumental undertaking, and because all of the beads are not equal in size, she must cull just the right ones or her final piece will appear distorted in shape. Willits triumphs over all challenges in her reflective, stirring pilgrimage through color and light.

Journeys End | 2003 ▶

20½ x 9½ x ¾ inches
(52.1 x 24.1 x 1.9 cm)
Seed beads; loom woven

Photo by Philip Arny

▲ **Main Street: Somewhere in the West** | 2005

11¾ x 13 x ¾ inches (29.8 x 33 x 1.9 cm)

Seed beads; loom woven

Photo by Philip Arny

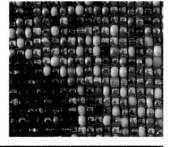

A Maze | 2002 ▼

18 x 16 x ⅜ inches
(45.7 x 40.6 x 1 cm)
Seed beads; loom woven

Photos by Philip Arny

" Since I was a very young artist I've been trying to get onto paper, film, fabric, or beadweaving a mood or sensation that has overtaken me in places, or in mental or emotional states, where I feel I'm in the presence of the, oh, I just this minute understand it—the Deity! Of course, I can't depict Godness, nor would I want to—the experience being so different for each person—but I can try to transmit, reflect, and be a conduit for the way things looked just a few minutes before Someone appeared. "

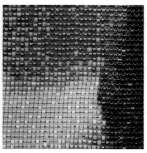

◀ Arches Gap | 2005

20 x 13¾ x ¾ inches
(50.8 x 34.9 x 1.9 cm)
Seed beads; loom woven

Photos by Philip Arny

Nine | 2002 ▶

12 x 18¾ x ⅜ inches
(30.5 x 47.6 x 1 cm)
Seed beads; loom woven

Photo by Philip Arny

▲ **Junction** | 2002

16½ x 13½ x ⅜ inches (41.9 x 34.3 x 1 cm)
Seed beads; loom woven
Photos by Philip Arny

" I've always been
intoxicated by the effects
of light against dark and
dark against light. It fills
me with joy to follow
a gradation from the
brightness to the shadows.
Color is delicious to
me, too, but *value* is the
structure of my work.
From this you may be able
to tell that I was educated
as a printmaker. "

◀ **City North of Home** | 2002

15 x 17¾ x ⅜ inches (38.1 x 45.1 x 1 cm)
Seed beads; loom woven

Photo by Philip Arny

◀ **Perch** | 2000

12½ x 15½ x ⅜ inches
(31.8 x 39.4 x 1 cm)
Seed beads; loom woven

Photo by Philip Arny

" One of the goals of an artist, as I was taught in art school, is to alter—hopefully for the better—the way in which the viewer of one's work perceives the world. We can argue whether this is a good goal or not. But I am lucky enough to have a few friends who claim to have experienced 'Laura-vision,' seeing the real world in terms of my work. So, I can claim to have altered at least some people's perceptions. "

◀ **En Trance** | 2002
19¾ x 15½ x ⅜ inches
(50.2 x 39.4 x 1 cm)
Seed beads; loom woven
Photo by Philip Arny

Later | 2003

14¾ x 16¾ x ¾ inches
(37.5 x 42.5 x 1.9 cm)
Seed beads; loom woven

Photo by Philip Arny

A Room | 2005 ▶

9 x 6½ x ¾ inches
(22.9 x 16.5 x 1.9 cm)
Seed beads; loom woven

Photo by Philip Arny

Ann Tevepaugh Mitchell

THE HUMAN CONDITION expressed in beadwork: From the joy and excitement of seeing a special bird in *The Birdwatcher*, to the despair and sense of devastating loss in *Kosovo*, Ann Tevepaugh Mitchell's sculptures capture the wide range of human experience. She puts emotion inside each piece, and takes viewers to the place where the scene is set, expanding their awareness beyond the sculpture itself. A master manipulator of peyote stitch, Mitchell increases and decreases at the correct times to create compelling figures. Color plays an important role in her work; Mitchell's color choices add depth to her vision. In *Morning Light*, the color seems frail, the skin texture loose. The solemn work prompts introspection, for viewers to think about age: Where has the time gone? Have I made the right choices in my life? Each piece by Mitchell tells a story—whether hers or your own—that moves viewers far beyond the work itself.

◀ **Wading In** │ 2003

16 x 10 x 7 inches (40.6 x 25.4 x 17.8 cm)
Seed beads, thread; peyote stitch
Photos by Dean Powell

" Ideas for my figures appear as pictures to me when I first wake up in the morning, before speaking. I work directly from those images, without any sketches or graphs. The challenge of working improvisationally is that I am joining what is already constructed with what is still in my imagination. Doing so requires total concentration. I cannot talk while I am working, although I do listen to music. "

▲ Kosovo | 2002

12 x 12 x 9 inches (30.5 x 30.5 x 22.9 cm)
Seed beads, thread, stones, glass bottles; peyote
stitch, right-angle weave, embellishment
Photos by Dean Powell

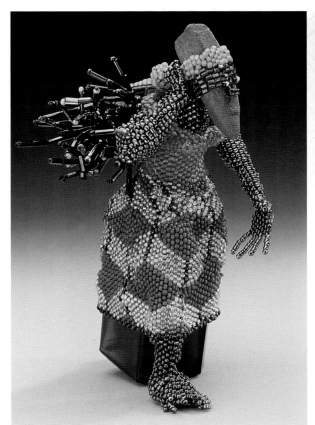

▲ **Refugees** | 1997

6 x 5 x 4 inches (15.2 x 12.7 x 10.2 cm) each
Seed beads, thread, stones, apothecary bottles;
random count peyote stitch

Photos by Dean Powell

The Birdwatcher | 2000 ▶

15 x 8 x 6 inches (38.1 x 20.3 x 15.2 cm)
Seed beads, thread, rocks; random count
peyote stitch, random netting, fringe,
right-angle weave

Photo by Dean Powell

The Perm | 1996 ▶

20 x 14 x 12 inches
(50.8 x 35.6 x 30.5 cm)
Seed beads, thread;
random count
peyote stitch

Photos by Dean Powell

◀ **Morning Light** | 1993

7 x 7 x 5 inches
(17.8 x 17.8 x 12.7 cm)
Seed beads, thread,
stone; peyote stitch

Photos by Dean Powell

▲ **Evening Star** | 1993

11 x 4 x 4 inches (27.9 x 10.2 x 10.2 cm)
Seed beads, thread; peyote stitch

Photos by Dean Powell

" Using a needle and thread has been natural to me since my mother taught me to sew as a little girl. Making things with our hands was something we did a lot of at home. Although I studied artistic anatomy in art school, I think my realistic approach to beadwork figures was influenced by the way my mother taught me to make donut and sausage men. Head = large donut. Arm = two sausages joined at elbow. Hand = small donut. Etc. "

" Sometimes when I look at a figure I've just finished, I have no idea how I did it. I can hardly remember the many months of making and joining small sections, analyzing posture and proportion, figuring out balance, imagining feeling and expression; of threading countless needles, straightening bent needles, waxing threads, mixing up beads, sorting them out, sweeping them off the floor. I just look at the figure and think, 'I know you!' "

▲ **Bathing Beauty No. 1** | 1998
17 x 7 x 9 inches (43.2 x 17.8 x 22.9 cm)
Seed beads, thread, glass, shell, dried and preserved kelp stem; peyote stitch, netting
Photo by Dean Powell

▼ Dumbbell | 1997

13 x 5 x 4 inches (33 x 12.7 x 10.2 cm)
Seed beads, thread, rocks; peyote stitch, fringe
Photo by Dean Powell

▲ Flute Player | 1998

17 x 12 x 10 inches (43.2 x 30.5 x 25.4 cm)
Seed beads, thread, glass; peyote stitch
Photo by Dean Powell

Marcia DeCoster

COLOR CHOICES COMBINE with shape design and the use of different sizes of beads in the exuberant work of Marcia DeCoster. The viewer's eye is drawn round and round her beaded jewelry, partly by the seeming movement of the pieces themselves. Sometimes her colors are bright, as in *Ringlets*, while a piece like *Victoria* is somewhat more subdued in color choices. *Quadrille Medaglia* is a skillful example of jewelry—and interest—that is created by employing different sizes and shapes of beads. DeCoster's expertise in single-needle right-angle weave allows her great freedom of expression in creating three dimensional shapes. *Rings of Saturn* and *Urchin Lariat* are wonderful testaments to what DeCoster's mind and hands can produce when playing with physical dimensions. She communicates her joy about beadweaving—as well as her knowledge and bold vision—in every piece.

▲ **Quadrille Medaglia** | 2007
7½ x ¾ x ⅓ inches (19.1 x 1.9 x 0.9 cm)
Seed beads, crystals, cubes, crystal flowers, crystal squares; woven medallion
Photo by artist

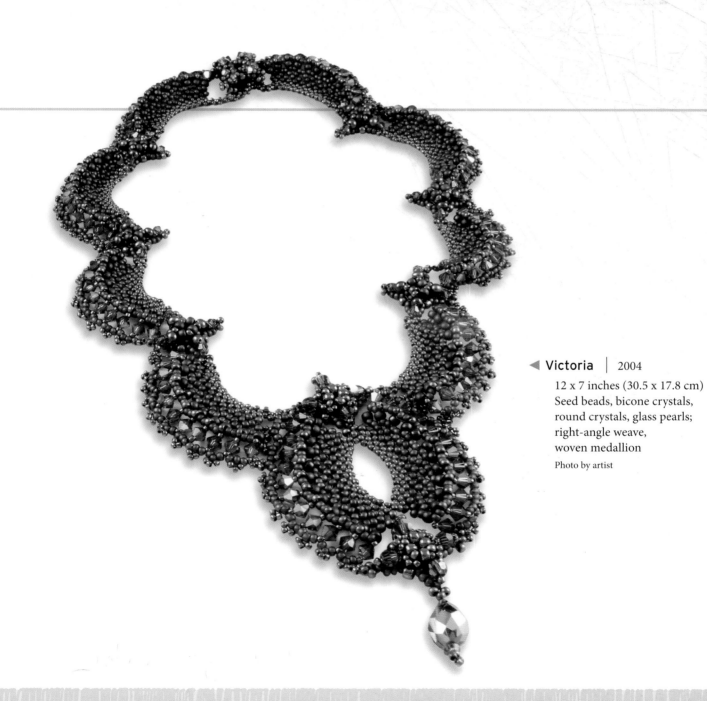

◄ **Victoria** | 2004

12 x 7 inches (30.5 x 17.8 cm)
Seed beads, bicone crystals,
round crystals, glass pearls;
right-angle weave,
woven medallion

Photo by artist

▲ **Urchin Lariat** | 2007

4 x 2 x 2 inches (10.2 x 5.1 x 5.1 cm)
Seed beads, crystals, glass accent beads;
right-angle weave, netting, embellishment
Photo by artist

▲ **Crystal Collage** | 2004

10 x 4 x ¼ inches (25.4 x 10.2 x 0.6 cm)
Seed beads, crystals, fire-polished beads;
right-angle weave, embellishment
Photo by artist

◀ **Tesserae** | 2007

5 x 2 x ¼ inches (12.7 x 5.1 x 0.6 cm)
Seed beads, crystals, Chinese cord;
right-angle weave, peyote stitch bezel

Photos by artist

" Certain pieces I see complete in my mind before picking up needle and beads. I know exactly how I will execute the design. Other pieces evolve through trial and error, using a particular stitch or combination of stitches, as I realize my vision. Still others start out with an implicit understanding that I will change and improve them along the way. The element of surprise is a large part of the joy for me, as bracelets become anklets, lacy fans become earrings, and necklaces become lariats. **"**

◀ **Rings of Saturn** | 1999

4 x 2 x 2 inches (10.2 x 5.1 x 5.1 cm)
Seed beads, cylinder seed beads,
glass accent beads; right-angle
weave, peyote stitch

Photos by artist

◀ **Beaded Bangles** | 2005

½ x 4 x ½ inches (1.3 x 10.2 x 1.3 cm)
Seed beads, squares, crystals, rubber armature;
right-angle weave, embellishment

Photo by artist

▲ **Ringlets** | 1998

2 x 2 x ¼ inches (5.1 x 5.1 x 0.6 cm)
Seed beads; right-angle
weave, embellishment

Photos by artist

" I gravitate toward beadweaving
using single-needle right-angle
weave because of the amazing
diversity of this stitch. I'm able
to create supple ropes, a draped
fabric, or a self-supporting structure
depending on how a piece is woven
and embellished. "

―――――――――

Cappadocia Cuff | 2007

7½ x 4 x ¼ inches (19.1 x 10.2 x 0.6 cm)
Seed beads, crystals, fire-polished
beads; right-angle weave

Photo by artist

Etruscan Treasure | 2006 ▶

3 x 2 x ¼ inches (7.6 x 5.1 x 0.6 cm)
Seed beads, crystals, Swarovski Rivoli
crystal, gold toggle clasp; right-angle
weave, peyote stitch, spiral necklace

Photo by artist

MARCIA DeCOSTER

" I experienced a breakthrough when I realized that creation is a process, and that it might take several prototypes before I'm satisfied with the result. Once I discovered this, it became easier to explore options. Letting go of a particular outcome, I really can enjoy the process of creativity, and so my work has been enhanced. "

◀ **My Secret Garden** | 2000

5 x 2 x 2 inches (12.7 x 5.1 x 5.1 cm)
Seed beads, fire-polished beads, glass
flowers, anodized aluminum rings,
lampworked beads by Lisa Niven
Kelly; right-angle weave, peyote
stitch, fringe, spiral necklace
Photos by artist

Joyce J. Scott

COMBINE IMPROVISATIONAL peyote stitch, a plate of mixed-up beads, and political and social commentary, and you have the work of Joyce J. Scott. Her creative gift flows from a background rich in visual and performance arts, and she is tireless in her efforts to pass her knowledge and spark along. Scott unlocks the beaded dimensional figure and risks the chance of doing something new. *Heard It Through the Grapevine*, a wearable narrative, offers challenging dimensions not only physically with the piece itself but also in the emotional content of its story. When viewers look at the work, that first visual punch makes them begin to study the script of what is being said. They then have to listen to their own internal reactions to decipher what they are to learn. Scott is a fearless innovator who breaks down all barriers, and there isn't a challenge too big when it comes to her ingenious art. The proof? She transformed her beadwoven piece *Lips* into an 18-foot mosaic installation at a major airport!

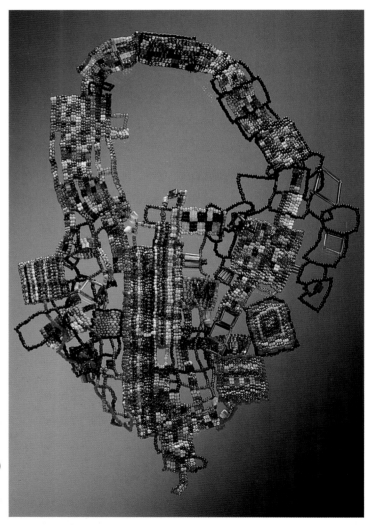

Stripes | 2003 ▶

13 x 10 inches (33 x 25.4 cm)
Seed beads, thread; peyote
stitch with variations

Photo by Norman Watkins

Lips | 1992 ▶

18 x 10 x 4 inches (45.7 x 25.4 x 10.2 cm)
Seed beads, thread, wire; peyote
stitch with variations

Photos by Kanji Takeno

▲ Mosaic

▲ Purple Monkeys │ 2001

20 x 16 x 8 inches (50.8 x 40.6 x 20.3 cm)
Glass bottle, seed beads, thread, wire;
peyote stitch with variations

Photo by Norman Watkins

▼ Mammy, Martini and Miss Ann │ 2000

14 x 10 inches (35.6 x 25.4 cm)
Seed beads, thread; peyote stitch with variations

Photo by Norman Watkins

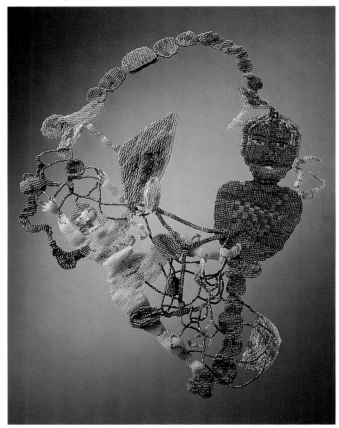

" The creation of art is my testimony to life and from it my blessings flow. I've been given great gifts, and I'm not stupid enough to believe they came only from me. I come from a long line of African-American artists who alchemized their environs without thoughts of great fame. Cotton pickers who bartered for the fabrics woven in the local mills from fiber they picked. Crocheters, quilters, weavers, potters, blacksmiths, singers, and storytellers all have coalesced in me. "

◄ **Heard It Through the Grapevine** │ 2005

12 x 9 x 2½ inches (30.5 x 22.9 x 6.4 cm)
Seed beads, thread, wire, glass inclusions,
photographs; peyote stitch with variations
Photo by Norman Watkins

JOYCE J. SCOTT

▼ **Lovers** | 2002

14 x 10 x 1½ inches (35.6 x 25.4 x 3.8 cm)
Seed bead, thread, wire; peyote stitch with variations
Photo by Norman Watkins

▲ **Yeller Girl** | 2006

25 x 10 x 9 inches (63.5 x 25.4 x 22.9 cm)
Seed beads, wire, thread, African sculpture;
peyote stitch with variations
Photo by Norman Watkins

" My work envelops beauty—the desire to luxuriate in it and show pride in the skill of it, from the making to the looking. I'm addicted to it. The true risk for me is to blend beauty and message by negotiating the road between them— sometimes falling into the rut, and then retrieving myself through dedication, humor, and believing that things can change for the better if people are challenged. "

◀ **I Left My Wife For Her** | 2004
14 x 9 x 3 inches (35.6 x 22.9 x 7.6 cm)
Seed beads, thread; peyote
stitch with variations
Photo by Norman Watkins

JOYCE J. SCOTT

" Stand stiff-backed and smiling as the gift of art defies inanity and the death of spirit. I am blessed. I glow. This is not bragging. This is the pride that comes from knowing my folks hid their lights, lied about their intelligence and beauty. Ate dung to give me butter. I will never stop working. My hunger for origination, my mother's care, and having no money ensure that. I persevere and then knock everybody's socks off with the products of my endeavors."

◀ **Comet** | 2000

12 x 12 x 5 feet (3.7 x 3.7 x 1.5 meters)
Seed beads, wire, thread, metal base,
illuminated globes covered with beads
on coal; peyote stitch with variations
Photo by artist

◀ Howdy Doody on Crack Imagines His
Baby Photo | 2005

    16 x 2 x 8 inches (40.6 x 5.1 x 20.3 cm)
    Ceramic and glass seed beads, thread;
    peyote stitch with variations

    Photo by Norman Watkins

◀ Believe I've Been Sanctified | 1991

    17 x 15 x 13 feet (5.2 x 4.6 x 4 meters)
    Seed beads, wood, thread, wire, mixed
    media; peyote stitch with variations

    Photos by John McWilliams

JOYCE J. SCOTT

Jeanette Ahlgren

FROM THE TIME she first loomed beads on an antique potholder loom in 1976 to today, when her signature wire-beaded vessels are widely renowned, Jeanette Ahlgren has been exploring her world through color and shape. Two distinct image styles shine through: One employs sharp, bright graphic elements and joyous colors, and the other opens up realistic windows into Ahlgren's own reality by its pointillistic renderings. Each style conveys a mood and a way in, helping viewers get emotionally closer to the artist's vision. Reds and yellows are set against blues and purples to open a vessel up visually, as does the actual shape of the work. The playfulness of the shapes invites closer inspection.

Ahlgren's realistic images, like the road and forest in *The Road Home*, are all about introspection. Grounded with black or white framing, these vessels are self-contained natural worlds, and viewers are asked to see beyond their surfaces. The simplicity of all Ahlgren's magnificent structures eliminates distractions and helps viewers pause to reflect on their own journeys.

▲ **Regrowth** | 1994
12 x 12 x 7 inches (30.5 x 30.5 x 17.8 cm)
Seed beads, wire; loom woven
Photo by artist

◀ **Stretch** | 2007

18 x 13 x 13 inches
(45.7 x 33 x 33 cm)
Seed beads, wire;
loom woven

Photo by artist

▲ **V12** | 2000

13 x 12 x 12 inches (33 x 30.5 x 30.5 cm)
Seed beads, wire; loom woven

Photo by artist

▲ **Sunny Blue** | 2000

12 x 12 x 8 inches (30.5 x 30.5 x 20.3 cm)
Seed beads, wire; loom woven

Photo by artist

▲ **Extensions** | 1997

15 x 15 x 15 inches (38.1 x 38.1 x 38.1 cm)
Seed beads, wire; loom woven

Photo by artist

" In order to avoid trouble with color, I first try to decide what one color does not go with the mood or subject I'm trying to convey. I then throw that color—along with its relatives—out. For some reason, this missing color makes all the other colors I've decided to use that much more precious. This helps the final structure communicate, and also forces me out of any cushy color ruts."

JEANETTE AHLGREN

" Wire weaving takes about three times as long as beadweaving with thread. When I'm trying to finish four new structures for a show, it's common for me to be at the loom for 10 hours a day, six days a week, for at least five months straight. For this reason, I do not watch TV. "

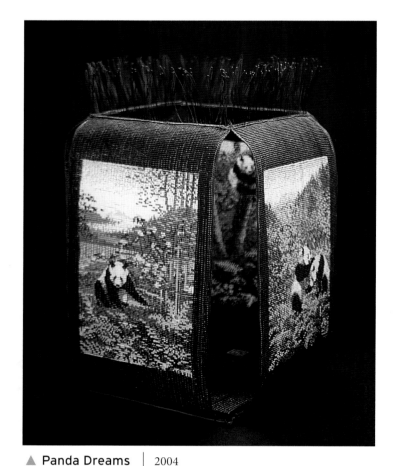

▲ **Panda Dreams** | 2004
15 x 10 x 10 inches (38.1 x 25.4 x 25.4 cm)
Cylinder seed beads, wire; loom woven
Photo by artist

▲ **The Road Home** | 2003

14 x 11 x 11 inches (35.6 x 27.9 x 27.9 cm)
Cylinder seed beads, wire; loom woven

Photos by artist

" Roughs that I work from are full size, in color, and as perfected as possible before I even buy beads. Sometimes I will make a full-size paper mockup of a piece if I'm concerned about a bad tangency. Wire weaving takes a lot of time, and to have to rip out something that isn't working can set you back at least a day, which can put anyone in a rather crabby mood. **"**

Something in Red | 2001 ▶
13 x 10½ x 10½ inches
(33 x 26.7 x 26.7 cm)
Seed beads, wire; loom woven
Photo by artist

◀ **Tea in the Garden** | 1999

11 x 8½ x 8½ inches (27.9 x 21.6 x 21.6 cm)
Cylinder seed beads, seed beads, wire; loom woven

Photo by artist

Second Childhood | 2002 ▶

12 x 12½ x 12½ inches
(30.5 x 31.8 x 31.8 cm)
Seed beads, wire; loom woven

Photo by artist

Natasha St. Michael

A PROPHETIC TITLE—*Oh the Webs We Weave*—graced the first beadwoven piece made by Natasha St. Michael. One idea leads to another for this self-taught weaver, and a wonderful creative body of work is the happy result. Organic life forms are conjured from beads and her imagination. The incredible textures and visual movement St. Michael creates with peyote stitch are astonishing. Simple individual structures—made from seed beads of different shapes and sizes—grow into hanging or surface works of art. The titles of her pieces are so apropos that I wonder which came first, the title or St. Michael's vision of each piece. I look at *Fragmented* and can't help but speculate where and when the next colony will break off and start growing on its own. *Thriving* virtually breathes—the shapes she's made and colors she's chosen bring the piece to life as a one and a many. St. Michael's work is fresh and original.

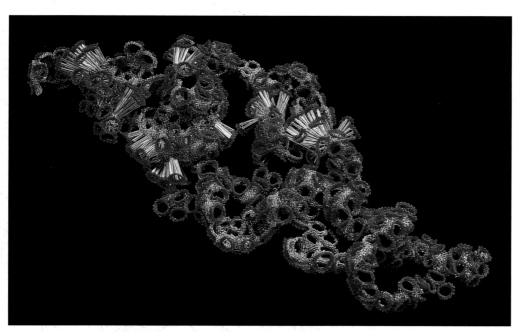

◀ **Carcass** | 2005
21¼ x 10¼ x 3⅛ inches
(54 x 26 x 8 cm)
Cylinder seed beads,
seed beads, glass bugle
beads, nylon thread;
peyote stitch
Photo by Paul Litherland

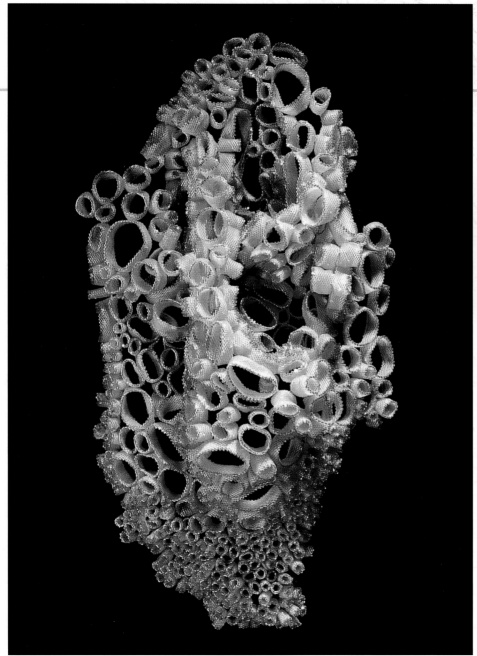

◀ **Thriving** │ 2007

20 x 13 x 5½ inches
(51 x 33 x 14 cm)
Glass beads, nylon
thread; hand woven

Photos by Paul Litherland

▲ **Sprouting** | 2007

29½ x 16½ x 4¾ inches (75 x 42 x 12 cm)
Cylinder seed beads, seed beads,
nylon thread; peyote stitch

Photos by Paul Litherland

" My inspiration comes from microbiology—everything from cellular structures beneath the skin to organic elements found on the ocean floor. I am intrigued by the life cycles of living matter; the process of growing, spreading, and multiplying; and the ever-present reality of mutation, transformation, and decay. My passion, as well as my challenge, is to represent organic matter in a state of perpetual growth or in the stages of its demise. "

▲ **Ferment** | 2002

23³⁄₁₆ x 19¼ x 6¼ inches (59 x 49 x 16 cm)
Seed beads, cylinder seed beads,
nylon thread, metal wire; peyote stitch

Photos by Paul Litherland

Fissure | 2005 ▶

16⅛ x 11 x 1¹⁵⁄₁₆ inches (41 x 28 x 5 cm)
Cylinder seed beads, seed
beads, glass bugle beads,
nylon thread; peyote stitch

Photos by Paul Litherland

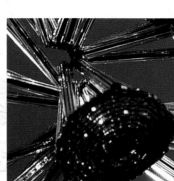

" When I start an artwork I have an idea about how I'll assemble it, but I don't weave it together until the end. I weave the hundreds of forms that make up the piece, sometimes laying them out as I work along, sometimes putting them aside in a bowl or a bag until I'm ready to put them together. Weaving the piece together is the most frightening and exciting time—it's the time of uncertainty about whether the piece will work or not. "

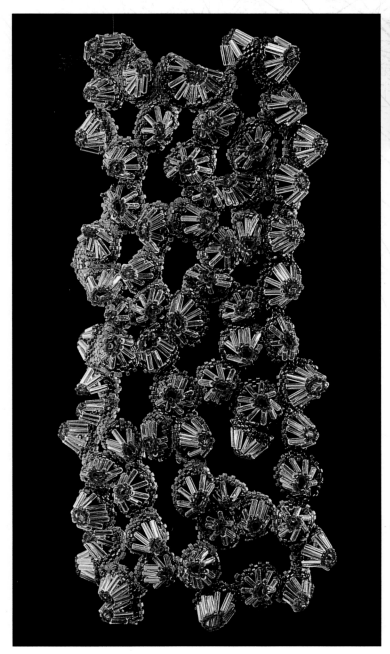

◄ **Germinate** | 2003
9¹/₁₆ x 5½ x 1 inches
(23 x 14 x 2.5 cm)
Glass bugle beads,
cylinder seed beads,
nylon thread;
peyote stitch
Photos by Paul Litherland

▲ **Fragmented** | 2004

21¼ x 11 x 2⅜ inches (54 x 28 x 6 cm)
Cylinder seed beads, seed beads,
nylon thread; peyote stitch

Photo by Paul Litherland

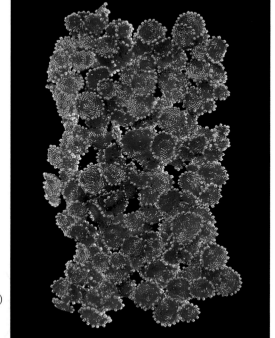

Piles | 2003 ▶

12³⁄₁₆ x 8⅝ x 1 inches (31 x 22 x 2.5 cm)
Cylinder seed beads, seed beads,
nylon thread; peyote stitch

Photo by Paul Litherland

" My background and education were in contemporary fiber arts, but I found the flat surface of textiles too limiting. I was yearning to create more three-dimensional structures, to play with surface and texture, and simultaneously to incorporate my fascination with the dynamic interaction of transparent color—all of which brought me to the beads. I use one beadweaving technique: peyote stitch. It's the only beadweaving technique I know, and even today I'm amazed at what can be produced by this one stitch. "

▲ **Oh the Webs We Weave** | 1999
24 x 20¹/₁₆ x ⅜ inches (61 x 51 x 1 cm)
Seed beads, nylon thread; peyote stitch
Photo by Jocelyn Blais

Amolia Willowsong

WHEN YOU LOOK at the beadwork of Amolia Willowsong, it feels like you've come home. Nature surrounds you with her tender arms. Willowsong takes incredible gemstones, backs them with leather, and bezels them with peyote stitch using her signature bronze seed beads. Her refined technique never overpowers the natural beauty of the stones or pearls she employs. The stones, placed asymmetrically, are then brought together with a freeform peyote technique that Willowsong makes all her own. The shapes are organic, and the eye moves from one place to another in surveying each piece's visual softness and receptivity. Willowsong's compositional wisdom is evident throughout her work; she knows when to leave negative space and when to deepen or lighten the colors of the beads. Her intuition and process are demonstrated to great effect in *Butterfly Dreams* and *Mango Salsa Sunset*. Willowsong's jewelry makes for wondrous, wearable works of art.

Sipping Mimosa's Neckpiece and Earrings | 2007 ▶

Neckpiece, 18 x 1¼ x ¾ inches (45.7 x 3.2 x 1.9 cm); earrings, 2 x ½ inches (5 x 1.2 cm) each
Seed beads, Tampa Bay coral drusy, freshwater pearls, faceted lemon quartz teardrops, deer hide, Russian stichtite; freeform peyote stitch
Photo by Tim Barnwell

◀ **Butterfly Dreams** │ 2007

> 19 x 1¾ x 1½ inches (48.3 x 4.4 x 3.8 cm)
> Seed beads, deer hide, freshwater pearls,
> faceted watermelon tourmaline, carved
> jasper leaves; freeform peyote stitch
>
> Photo by Tim Barnwell

▲ Mango Salsa Sunset │ 2007

18 x 1¼ x 1¼ inches (45.7 x 3.2 x 3.2 cm)
Seed beads, deer hide, rainbow pyrite, carved carnelian
leaf, amber, freshwater pearls; freeform peyote stitch

Photo by Tim Barnwell

▼ Twilight Wisteria │ 2007

21 x 1¾ inches (53.3 x 4.4 cm)
Seed beads, Brazilian amethyst cluster, purple
titanium drusy, raven black freshwater pearls,
deer hide; freeform peyote stitch

Photo by Tim Barnwell

" The name Willowsong was given to me by two Native American women who were my teachers in beadwork and more. They inspired and encouraged me to think about bringing beauty into the world in every way possible. They said that in the old ways every bead was a prayer said for the future wearer of your weaving. "

▲ **Crystalline Gardens** | 2007

17 x 1¼ inches (43.2 x 3.2 cm)
Seed beads, Herkimer diamond, abalone,
deer hide, Swarovski crystals, pearls,
freeform peyote stitch, art nouveau stitch
Photo by Tim Barnwell

▲ **In Monet's Garden** | 2007

18 x 2¾ inches (45.7 x 7 cm)
Seed beads, Argentina rhodochrosite
cabochon; peyote stitch
Photo by Tim Barnwell

> " A new weaving begins with a gemstone, one with depth of color and texture. Rough, natural clustered stones are my favorite. Next, I add a few gradated colors of seed beads to enhance the stones. I have no plan really. I am excited by the blending of beads and stones and the shapes that form as I weave. "

▲ **Red Coral Neckpiece** | 2006

18 x 1½ inches (48.3 x 3.8 cm)
Seed beads, deer hide, branch coral,
gold keshi pearls, freshwater pearls;
freeform peyote stitch

Photo by Tim Barnwell

▲ **Rhodolite Sculptural Elements Bracelet** | 2006

7 x 1¾ inches (17.8 x 4.4 cm)
Seed beads, deer hide, rhodolite, Russian stichtite,
freshwater pearls; freeform peyote stitch,
sculptural elements technique

Photo by Tim Barnwell

▲ Willow's Song │ 2007

18 x 2 x 1½ inches (45.7 x 5.1 x 3.8 cm)
Seed beads, deer hide, faceted peridot,
Russian stichtite, freshwater pearls;
freeform peyote stitch, backstitch

Photo by Tim Barnwell

▼ Meditation │ 2007

20 x 1¼ inches (50.8 x 3.2 cm)
Seed beads, deer hide, Chilean chrysocolla,
abalone; peyote stitch, brick stitch, backstitch

Photo by Tim Barnwell

" Beading all these years has taught me to see everything around me in greater detail. I notice what colors appear in the highlights and shadows and what gives character and contrast to my surroundings. I like the weavings to be as textured as the garden—the leaves and flowers varied and vibrant. I see graceful gradations of colors playing next to each other, wanting to come alive in the weavings. "

Elsya's Wishes | 2006 ▶

16 x 1¼ x 1½ inches (40.6 x 3.2 x 3.8 cm)
Seed beads, blue titanium drusy, abalone, freshwater pearls, deer hide; freeform peyote stitch
Photo by Tim Barnwell

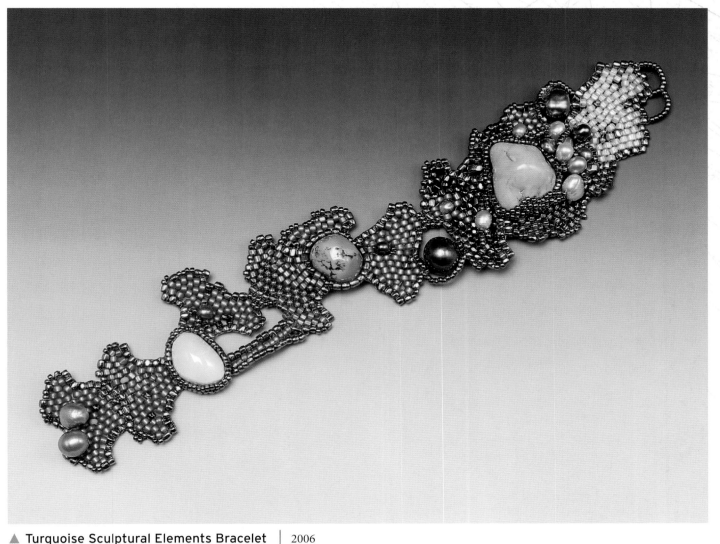

▲ **Turquoise Sculptural Elements Bracelet** | 2006

7 x 2 inches (17.8 x 5.1 cm)
Seed beads, deer hide, turquoise, pearls,
crystals; sculptural elements technique

Photo by Tim Barnwell

Linda Fifield

EARTH, WATER, WIND, and fire—all the elements of nature—spring to life in the beadworked vessels of Linda Fifield. These pieces speak their own names and beckon for closer inspection. A ruffled fire in *Earth Ablaze* is cooled only by its beauty. In *Stars Out*, the heavens hover above the Earth, separate and connected all at once. Fifield stitches beads in place one at a time, capturing every nuance she designs. Working around wooden vessels she turns herself, she covers the wood with Czech glass seed beads that become more than the sum of their parts—they are extensions of this woman's inner being, a place where beauty grows and responds to her inner stillness. Fifield's masterful beadwork dances with her world and universe, and takes viewers with her to the hills of rural Kentucky.

Earth Ablaze | 2002 ▶

8 x 4 x 4 inches (20.3 x 10.2 x 10.2 cm)
Seed beads, hollowed wooden
vessel; gourd stitch
Photo by Jack T. Fifield

◀ **Earth, Water, Wind and Fire #13** │ 2003

8 x 3½ x 3½ inches (20.3 x 8.9 x 8.9 cm)
Seed beads, hollowed wooden
vessel; gourd stitch

Photos by Jack T. Fifield

▲ **Heaven and Earth #16** | 2003

9½ x 5 x 5 inches (24.1 x 12.7 x 12.7 cm)
Seed beads, hollowed wooden vessel; gourd stitch

Photo by Jack T. Fifield

▲ **Earth Unfurling** | 1997

6 x 2½ x 2½ inches (15.2 x 6.4 x 6.4 cm)
Seed beads, hollowed wooden vessel,
walnut and maple lid; gourd stitch

Photo by Jack T. Fifield

" For generations my Appalachian family has made handwork an integral part of the daily rhythm of life. My life's path is a contemporary extension of that tradition. Stitching slowly, one bead at a time, allows for reflection. With each passing generation, the necessity to create objects has lessened, yet the desire to create remains. Today I create purely for the pleasure of creation. "

▲ **Fire Ring #6** | 2005
7 x 5 x 5 inches (17.8 x 12.7 x 12.7 cm)
Seed beads, hollowed wooden vessel; gourd stitch
Photo by Jack T. Fifield

▲ **Earth Landscape** | 2007
20 x 8 x 8 inches (50.8 x 20.3 x 20.3 cm)
Seed beads, bigleaf maple base; gourd stitch
Photo by Jack T. Fifield

" I live in the country with my eyes wide open to a wondrous environment, captive to the beauty and miracle of Mother Earth. The most influential person in my life was my granny, Mary Collins. My deep love for her kept me at her side often, mesmerized by her deft hands as she quilted, crocheted, or embroidered. Her patience and inner stillness had a profound effect on me. I often see her hands as I observe my own hands in motion. "

Earth and Fire #71 | 2001 ▶

18 x 7 x 7 inches (45.7 x 17.8 x 17.8 cm)
Seed beads, hollowed wooden
vessel; gourd stitch

Photo by Jack T. Fifield

◀ **Forest Floor** │ 1999

9 x 7 x 7 inches (22.9 x 17.8 x 17.8 cm)
Seed beads, freshwater pearls,
gemstones, redwood burl vessel,
bigleaf maple and ebony lid;
gourd stitch

Photos by artist

◀ **Stars Out** | 2006

17 x 6½ x 6½ inches (43.2 x 16.5 x 16.5 cm)
Seed beads, Texas ebony and bigleaf
maple vase; gourd stitch

Photos by Jack T. Fifield

" In 1974, a visit to The Field Museum in Chicago became a pivotal point in my life. I was spellbound by the finely woven baskets of Native American weavers. My fascination with Native American baskets led to a strong desire to create vessels of beauty and intricate structure. The skill, patience, and commitment necessary to create beaded vessels provide sustenance for my creative life. I often say, 'I'm not obsessed. I'm passionate!' "

Fire on the Mountain | 2002 ▶
7 x 4½ x 4½ inches (17.8 x 11.4 x 11.4 cm)
Seed beads, hollowed wooden vessel; gourd stitch
Photo by Jack T. Fifield

NanC Meinhardt

IMAGINATION COUPLED with insatiable longing is what you sense when you view NanC Meinhardt's work. Her great gift as an artist is her ability to look within and bring out her thoughts and emotions through her hands. And talented hands they are: Unafraid of trying new ideas the moment they come, Meinhardt is able to take a stitch and push its limits. Refusing to be restrained by the rules of conformity, she creates unique work prolifically. Meinhardt incorporates many off-loom stitches in her pieces, and she is best known for her free-form right-angle weave. As a teacher, she helps others actualize what she herself does best: finding and expressing a passionate creative voice. Being open to everything and loving the process are what NanC Meinhardt is all about.

Let Me In, Let Me Out Mask Series: Mother Load | 1996 ▶

12 x 8 x 4 inches (30.5 x 20.3 x 10.2 cm)
Seed beads, 22-karat-gold vintage seed beads, pressed glass beads, freshwater pearls, silk cord, nylon thread, wooden armature; freeform right-angle weave

Photo by Tom Van Eynde

◀ **Let Me In, Let Me Out Mask Series: Let Me In** | 1997

10 x 7½ x 4½ inches (25.4 x 19.1 x 11.4 cm)
Seed beads, pressed glass beads,
22-karat-gold seed beads, nylon
thread, silk cord, wooden armature;
freeform right-angle weave, encrusting

Photo by Tom Van Eynde

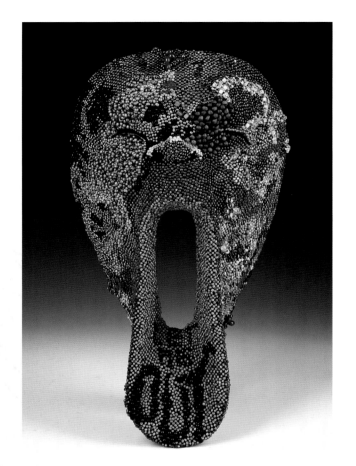

 Between a Rock and a Hard Place | 2001

12 x 8 x 5 inches (30.5 x 20.3 x 12.7 cm)
Seed beads, gold beads, freshwater pearls,
nylon thread, modeling compound, polymer
clay, terra cotta; freeform right-angle weave

Photo by Tom Van Eynde

▲ Let Me In, Let Me Out Mask Series:
Let Me Out | 1997

11 x 7½ x 4½ inches (27.9 x 19.1 x 11.4 cm)
Seed beads, pressed glass beads, nylon
thread, silk cord, wooden armature;
freeform right-angle weave, encrusting

Photo by Tom Van Eynde

▲ **Sssssnake** | 2001

10 x 24 x 8 inches (25.4 x 61 x 20.3 cm)
Seed beads, pressed glass beads, freshwater
pearls, semiprecious stones, wire mesh,
nylon thread; encrusting, applied beads

Photo by Tom Van Eynde

" I require and prefer solitude, yet making art allows
for such in-depth relationships: relationships with
the beads, my thoughts, my feelings, the colors that
surround me, and the work of my hands. When I'm with
my materials, there's so much to think about, to feel, to
discuss, and to do. People often ask how I find the time
to bead, but my problem isn't finding time to bead. My
problem is forcing myself to do anything else. "

▲ **Fable Vessel** | 1993

8½ x 15½ x 15 inches (21.6 x 39.4 x 38.1 cm)
Seed beads, cotton thread, muslin, silk thread, batting, nylon thread; brick stitch,
peyote stitch, two-drop peyote stitch, right-angle weave, bead embroidery
Photo by Tom Van Eynde

▲ Camouflage II | 2007

5½ x 5¾ x 6 inches (14 x 14.6 x 15.2 cm)
Seed beads, pressed glass beads, freshwater pearls, nylon thread;
brick stitch, peyote stitch, right-angle weave, encrusting
Photo by Tom Van Eynde

" I used to think feeling anxious—which is not the most comfortable feeling—was a sign something had gone terribly wrong with my beadwork. Now I understand an anxious feeling means I'm right on the edge of creating something new. This is both good and bad news. The bad news is there isn't any way around feeling anxious from time to time, as I long as I'm making art. The good news is I've developed a taste for it. "

NANC MEINHARDT

" You're working on your beadwork, and a question goes through your mind: 'I wonder what would happen if ... ?' What usually happens is you don't try to find out the answer to the 'what if' question, because you can't visualize the result. You can't visualize the result because you've never tried it, and another possibility floats away. But I believe if the idea was good enough to cross your mind, then it's worth exploring and finding out what would happen. "

◀ **Wander Anywhere You Wish** | 2000

22 x 19 x 1 inches (55.9 x 48.3 x 2.5 cm)
Seed beads, pressed glass beads, freshwater pearls, polymer clay, nylon thread; freeform right-angle weave, herringbone stitch
Photo by Tom Van Eynde

◀ **Hatching Rocks** │ 2005

10 x 14 inches (25.4 x 35.6 cm)
Seed beads, image transfer
medium, interfacing, satin,
nylon thread; embroidered
freeform right-angle weave

Photos by Tom Van Eynde

◀ **Miss Stitch** │ 1993

14 x 13½ x 1 inches (35.6 x 34.3 x 2.5 cm)
Seed beads, cotton thread, silk thread, interfacing,
silk, brocade, lace; bead embroidery, peyote stitch

Photo by Tom Van Eynde

Sonya Clark

COMMUNITY AND COMMUNICATION—two primal means of human connection—are great themes in the mesmerizing beadwork of Sonya Clark. Her series of peyote-stitched hands—simply representational, yet powerfully metaphorical—speaks with enormous archetypal resonance. Minimizing the distractions of excessive color or pattern variations, Clark's work directs viewers into oneness with her thoughts. The titles of her pieces give viewers additional insight into the artist's meanings. Pieces like *Promise*, *Reach*, and *Little Hug* carry and impart exceptional emotional resonance about what binds us together. Through her vibrant, powerful beadwork, Clark communicates human beings' basic yearnings both for singularity and to be part of a greater whole.

Promise | 2005 ▶

1 x 6 x 3 inches
(2.5 x 15.2 x 7.6 cm)
Seed beads; peyote stitch

Photo by Tom McInvaille

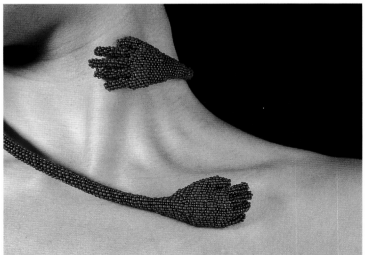

▲ **Little Hug** | 2002

3 x 6 x 6 inches (7.6 x 15.2 x 15.2 cm)
Seed beads, wire; peyote stitch

Photos by Tom McInvaille

" As archaeological heirlooms, beads remind us of our ancestors and genetic pool. Beads in abacuses and rosaries become mnemonics. I measure time, transfix gestures, celebrate cultural memory, and explore metaphor through the medium of beads. "

▲ **Eye to Eye** | 2001

2 x 6 x 6 inches (5.1 x 15.2 x 15.2 cm)
Cylinder seed beads, found frames;
peyote netting

Photos by Tom McInvaille

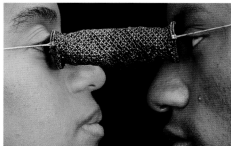

▲ **Golden Touch** | 2002

1 x 1 inch (2.5 x 2.5 cm) each
Seed beads; peyote stitch

Photo by Tom McInvaille

◀ **Climb** | 2005

180 x 12 inches
(457.2 x 30.5 cm)
Seed beads, wire;
peyote stitch

Photos by artist

" My hands have the unique wisdom of knowing beads. Early in the process of learning a technique, the head trains the hand, but eventually the hand becomes the master, and the head steps out of the process. My body understands the subtlety of its relationship with material and process in a way that is impossible for my head to imagine. "

Ras Blue | 1997 ▶

10 x 10 x 10 inches
(25.4 x 25.4 x 25.4 cm)
Seed beads, suede;
peyote stitch

Photos by Carole Harris

▲ **Offer** │ 2005

    15 x 6 x 6 inches (38.1 x 15.2 x 15.2 cm)

    Seed beads, metal; peyote stitch

    Photo by artist

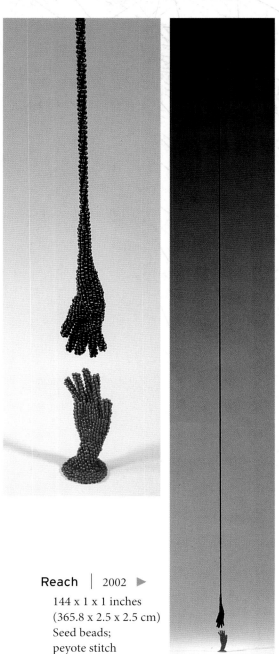

Reach │ 2002 ▶

    144 x 1 x 1 inches

    (365.8 x 2.5 x 2.5 cm)

    Seed beads;

    peyote stitch

    Photos by Tom McInvaille

SONYA CLARK

Holding Hands | 2005 ▶

1 x 9 x 6 inches
(2.5 x 22.9 x 15.2 cm)
Seed beads; peyote stitch
Photo by Tom McInvaille

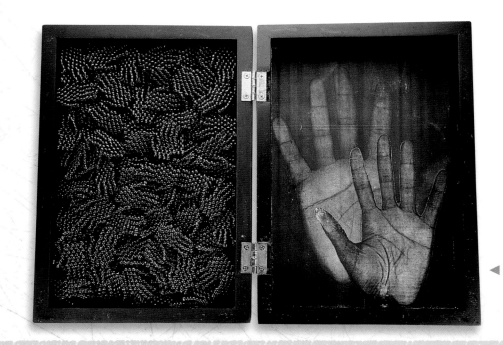

◀ **Handy** | 2002

2 x 12 x 6 inches (5.1 x 30.5 x 15.2 cm)
Seed beads, wooden box; peyote stitch
Photo by Tom McInvaille

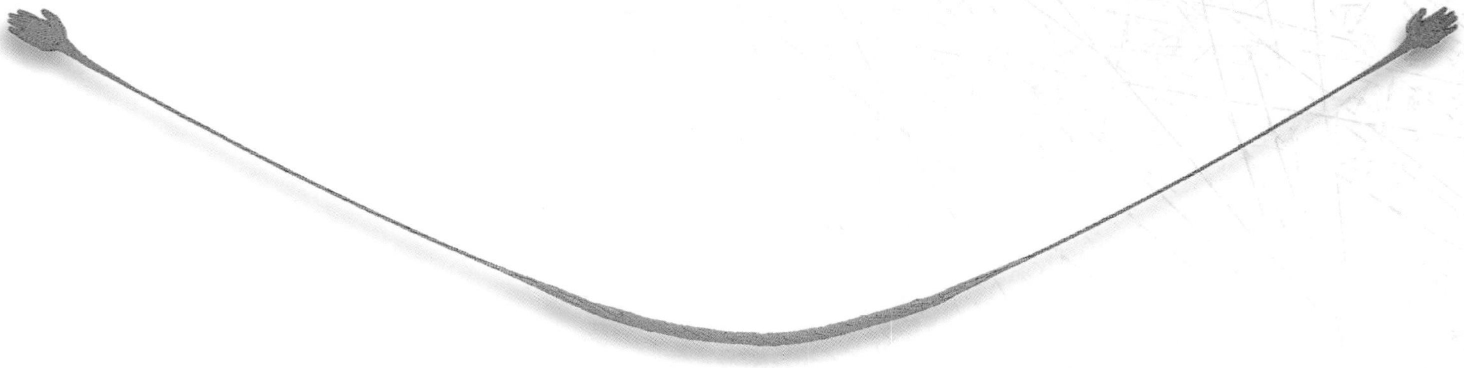

" With beads, it's all about the hole. Without it, beads cannot be strung or stitched together. The more beads in a piece, the less likely the beadwork will break—just as with communities, there's safety in numbers. The holes in beads are like the orifices we use to communicate. One to the next, beads are strung, as soundwaves connect us from mouth to ear. "

—————

Greet | 2005 ▶

24 x 72 inches (61 x 182.9 cm)
Seed beads; peyote stitch
Photos by Tom McInvaille

David K. Chatt

SINGLE-NEEDLE right-angle weave and David K. Chatt are nearly synonymous—thinking of one always brings the other to mind—but Chatt's work is emblematic of so much more. His creative genius delves into the depths of self-awareness, offering commentary and humor. As Chatt's sculptural visions dazzle, on a more straightforward level, regarding his beadwork itself, viewers reasonably might ask, "How does he *do* that?" *Confrontation in the Green Room* is a wonderful piece, not only for the emotional aspects it evokes but also for the style of the tableau. An everyday occurrence— looking in the mirror—is portrayed, the moment short-lived in real time but the thoughts of age and youth captured in that moment sure to expand throughout the character's day. In both its beadwork and its message, the piece's simple appearance belies a greater complexity, and viewers of a certain age can't help but empathize with the scenario portrayed. Chatt's compositional skills actualize his visionary thoughts in innovative artwork.

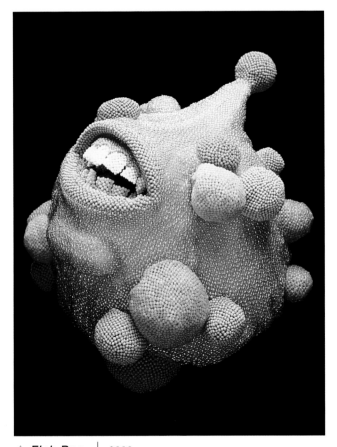

▲ **Flab Bag** | 2000

8 x 10 x 8 inches (20.3 x 25.4 x 20.3 cm)
Seed beads, acrylic spheres; right-angle weave
Photo by Larry Stesson

◀ **Artist in Residence** | 2001

9½ x 6 x 6 inches (24.1 x 15.2 x 15.2 cm)

Seed beads, wire armature; right-angle weave

Photos by Jim Maleki

" I've spent the past 20 years of my life stitching tiny bits of glass one to the next. As society has embraced the personal computer and many other life-changing, time-saving, world-rocking technologies, there I sit with needle, thread, and bead in hand, working to express myself in a medium that is time-consuming and tedious beyond reason. I'm not in prison, nor have I gone off my medication, so why do it? All I can tell you is that this is the work I'm compelled to do. "

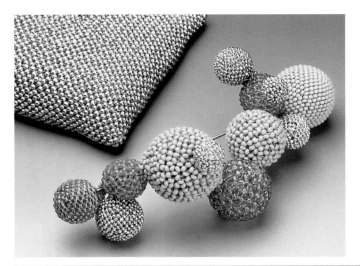

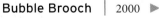

Bubble Brooch | 2000 ▶
5½ x 3½ x 3 inches
(14 x 8.9 x 7.6 cm)
Seed beads, armature made
from plastic beads and marbles;
right-angle weave
Photos by Harriet Burger

▲ **Hanging On By a Thread** | 1998
8 x 8 x 9 inches (20.3 x 20.3 x 22.9 cm)
Seed beads, glass marbles;
right-angle weave, peyote stitch
Photo by Larry Stesson

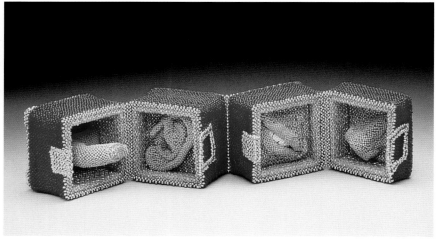

◀ **Portable Pink Parts** | 1998

2½ x 2½ x 6½ inches (6.4 x 6.4 x 16.5 cm)
Seed beads, armature made from bamboo skewers;
right-angle weave, peyote stitch

Photos by Larry Stesson

Breakfast Set | 2004 ▶

21 x 15 x 9 inches
(53.3 x 38.1 x 22.9 cm)
Seed beads, wire armature,
blown and lampworked glass;
right-angle weave, peyote stitch

Photos by Harriet Burger

" You can imagine how most parents would react if their 25-year-old son came to them and said, 'Hey, I've finally found something to do with my life. I'm going to string beads.' My mom didn't blink. She wanted all her children to be happy, productive, and decent. As a creative young person who had a hard time figuring it all out, her unfailing support and encouragement meant the world to me. "

◀ **Breaking News** │ 2001
4 x 6½ x 4 inches (10.2 x 16.5 x 10.2 cm)
Seed beads, wire armature;
right-angle weave
Photos by Harriet Burger

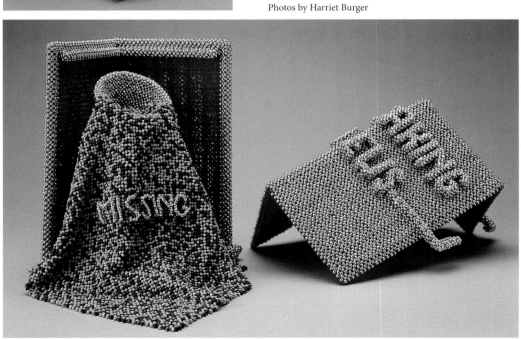

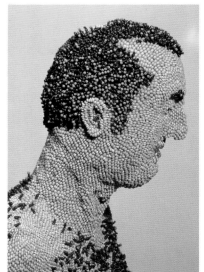

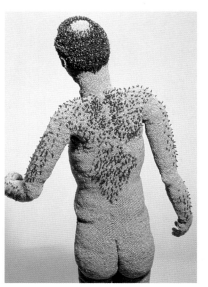

▲ **Confrontation in the Green Room** | 2004

14½ x 10 x 25 inches (35.6 x 25..4 x 63.5 cm)
Seed beads, armature made from metal
and fabric; peyote stitch, right-angle weave

Photos by Harriet Burger

Bubble Bowl | 1996 ▶

7 x 9 x 7 inches (17.8 x 22.9 x 17.8 cm)
Seed beads, wire armature wrapped
with bias tape; right-angle weave, fringe

Photo by Joe Manfredini

" I am a 6-foot, 4-inch white, American male, and as such I've grown up with certain societal expectations. I've always felt uncomfortable with the roles my culture has deemed appropriate for me. Any work that employs needle and thread is thought of as women's work, and with each technological development it's become increasingly unfashionable. To be male and working in such a laborious and gender-stereotyped medium in these times is part of what I endeavor to speak about in my work. "

White Men in Suits | 2002 ▶

25 x 7 x 13 inches (63.5 x 17.8 x 33 cm)
Seed beads, dollar bills, armature
by Leslie Campbell; right-angle
weave, peyote stitch
Photo by Harriet Burger

Rachel Nelson-Smith

CAN CHAOS BREED SERENDIPITY? In watching a movie, teaching her husband peyote stitch, and trying to recreate something she'd seen years before in her beading—all in one chaotic night—Rachel Nelson-Smith gave birth to the oothecal technique. She has turned her happy accident into a magnificent creative journey. The stitch is a combination of right-angle weave and even-count tubular peyote stitch. Nelson-Smith's creation looks like an egg carton, which explains the name—ootheca is the name of an insect egg case. The *Ootheca Cuff* series shows off the technique's dimensional form. The basic shape can be lengthened, as seen in *Sea Star Bangle longus*, or shortened, as in *Sea Star Bangle shortus*. It can become beaded beads—see *Oothecal Bede Necklace*—or a button, as in *Oothecal Button*. Nelson-Smith is always playing with different colors and shifting dimensions. And sometimes she takes a 180-degree turn and moves from tight control to freeform peyote stitch, as seen in *Bead Cruise*. The depth of Nelson-Smith's talents—like the voyage she takes viewers on—seems boundless.

Sea Star Bangle *shortus* | 2007 ▶

½ x 4½ x 4½ inches
(1.3 x 11.4 x 11.4 cm)
Japanese seed beads;
modified tubular right-angle weave,
tubular even-count peyote stitch

Photo by artist

▲ **Sea Star Bangle** *longus* | 2007

½ x 7½ x 7½ inches (1.3 x 19.1 x 19.1 cm)
Japanese seed beads; modified tubular right-angle weave, tubular even-count peyote stitch

Photo by artist

▼ **Oothecal Bede Necklace** | 2006

1⅛ x 7½ x 8½ inches (2.8 x 19.1 x 21.6 cm)
Japanese seed beads, Swarovski crystals,
glass lampworked beads by Lea Zinke,
Czech fire-polished glass beads, sterling
silver wire, flexible beading wire; tubular
modified right-angle weave, tubular
even-count peyote stitch, modified flat
even-count peyote stitch, bead stringing
Photos by artist

▼ Oothecal Button | 2006

1 x 1 x 1 inches (2.5 x 2.5 x 2.5 cm)
Japanese seed beads, Swarovski margarita crystal,
sterling silver wire; modified circular right-angle weave,
decreased tubular even-count peyote stitch, wire wrapping
Photos by artist

" With the encouragement of my Aunt Winny, I accepted being an artist and was able to move forward with my creative work. Until that admission, jewelry making was relegated to being a hobby. Why was I always late to the office? Why was I unhappy? Why did I hate my boss? In retrospect, the answer to these questions is obvious: I had yet to find my bead calling. "

◀ **Ootheca Cuff** *turqueise* │ 2006

1¾ x 3¼ x 3¼ inches (4.4 x 8.3 x 8.3 cm)
Japanese seed beads, Swarovski crystals, niobium wire,
sterling silver magnetic clasps; right-angle weave,
tubular even-count peyote stitch, basic weave

Photo by artist

Ootheca Cuff *aureat* │ 2006 ▶

1¾ x 3¼ x 3¼ inches (4.4 x 8.3 x 8.3 cm)
Japanese seed beads, Swarovski crystals,
gold-filled wire, gold-filled magnetic
clasps; right-angle weave, tubular even-
count peyote stitch, basic wire work

Photo by artist

◀ **Ootheca Cuff** *raspberry* │ 2006

1¾ x 3¼ x 3¼ inches (4.4 x 8.3 x 8.3 cm)
Japanese seed beads, Swarovski crystals,
sterling silver wire, sterling silver magnetic
clasps; right-angle weave, tubular even-
count peyote stitch, basic wire work

Photo by artist

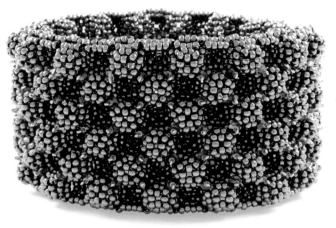

◄ **Ootheca Cuff** *gris* | 2007

1¾ x 3¼ x 3¼ inches (4.4 x 8.3 x 8.3 cm)
Japanese seed beads, Swarovski crystals,
sterling silver wire, sterling silver magnetic
clasps; right-angle weave, tubular even-
count peyote stitch, basic wire work

Photo by artist

" Jazz and jazz singing occupied my
informal studies in the late 1990s. I later
sang professionally, just as I was hired to
design jewelry. One of the most significant
realizations I made in both disciplines was
that I could create something new. In jazz,
it's called scatting. In beadweaving, I think
of it as changing from one stitch to another
stitch, or going sculptural—either way it's
improvisational. There is freedom with each
stitch taken and each note sung. "

▲ **Ootheca Cuff** *caterpillar* | 2007

1¾ x 3¼ x 3¼ inches (4.4 x 8.3 x 8.3 cm)
Japanese seed beads, Swarovski crystals,
sterling silver wire, sterling silver magnetic
clasps; right-angle weave, tubular even-
count peyote stitch, basic wire work

Photo by artist

RACHEL NELSON-SMITH

" Let go of the fear of making a mistake. Mistakes always can be ripped out, but they often lead to new possibilities. Let go of the fear of making something ugly. Often, something looks unattractive simply because it's new or in progress. If no more can be created, create more. When I believe I've come up with as much new design as I'm capable of, continuing to design yields work I previously would not have thought up. "

◀ **Bead Cruise** | 2007

3 x 3 x 1½ inches (7.6 x 7.6 x 3.8 cm)
Japanese seed beads, mother-of-pearl,
rose montees, freshwater pearls,
ceramic boat bead, Czech glass beads,
glass button; sculptural peyote stitch
Photo by artist

▲ **Pacific Waves** │ 2007

1¼ x 4¾ x 4¾ inches (3.2 x 12.1 x 12.1 cm)
Japanese seed beads, Czech glass druks, sterling
silver wire, sterling silver clasp; African helix,
bead embellishment, tubular even-count peyote
stitch, decreased tubular peyote over form

Photo by artist

Prickly Beaded Bead *green* │ 2006 ▶

⅝ x 5 x 8 inches (1.6 x 12.7 x 20.3 cm)
Japanese seed beads, Czech glass druks, Czech
lampworked glass beads, Swarovski crystal,
sterling silver wire; modified tubular even-count
peyote stitch, embellishment, wire wrapping

Photo by artist

Maggie Meister

THE BYZANTINE EMPIRE PROVIDES the inspiration for Maggie Meister's exquisite beaded jewelry. Each piece is artistically ornate, rich, and stylized. The hollow forms in *Persephone's Necklace*, for example, are beautifully structured and evidence Meister's fine expertise in tubular peyote stitch. Her choice of bead color also guides viewers down the ancient path, influenced by classic sensibilities. *Etruscan Cuff* captures the look of a golden, bejeweled bracelet; Meister weaves garnets into a three-drop peyote stitch base and then adds dimensional surface work and bezeled pearls. As she works out each new design, she chooses the best stitches for the job from the array she's mastered. Brick stitch and right-angle weave are perfect choices for *Solomon's Knot Bracelet*. Meister's impeccable work is immersed in the time period that inspires it, yet also offers leading-edge beadwork for our own time.

◀ **Hercules Knot Bracelet** | 2003

7½ x 1 x ¼ inches (19.1 x 2.5 x 0.6 cm)
Cylinder seed beads, seed beads, garnets, gold vermeil charms; right-angle weave, herringbone stitch, brick stitch, peyote stitch

Photo by Larry Sanders

▲ **Byzantine Collar** │ 2005

9½ x 9½ x ½ inches (24.1 x 24.1 x 1.2 cm)
Cylinder seed beads, Venetian gold foil beads,
freshwater pearls, chalcedony, amazonite;
peyote stitch, right-angle weave

Photo by Larry Sanders

Etruscan Cuff | 2004 ▶

7½ x 3 x ¼ inches (19.1 x 7.6 x 0.6 cm)
Cylinder seed beads, garnets,
freshwater pearls, gold-filled wire,
seed beads; three-drop peyote stitch,
brick stitch, square stitch
Photos by Tom Van Eynde

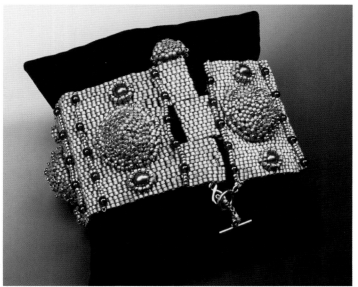

" I've always loved ancient
history. As a young girl, I went
to museums with my father.
When I see a mosaic or a piece
of ancient jewelry in a museum,
I want to capture that memory.
I'm inspired to create a piece
with seed beads using the design
or motif as a point of inspiration.
Seed beads are the medium I use
to recreate that moment. "

◀ Persephone's Necklace | 2006

7 x 9 x ½ inches (17.7 x 22.8 x 1.2 cm)
Cylinder seed beads, gold vermeil
beads, seed beads; circular peyote
stitch, tubular peyote stitch

Photo by Larry Sanders

MAGGIE MEISTER

▲ **Conchiglie Necklace** | 2004

11 x 7 x ⅛ inches (27.9 x 17.7 x 0.3 cm)
Cylinder seed beads, freshwater pearls;
right-angle weave, brick stitch

Photo by Tom Van Eynde

▲ **Santa Sofia Pendant** | 2006

3½ x 2 x 2 inches (8.9 x 5.1 x 5.1 cm)
Cylinder seed beads, freshwater pearls; peyote
stitch, right-angle weave, spiral rope chain

Photo by Larry Sanders

" I don't always make sketches of the pieces I want to make. I use the beads to draw them, trying different stitches to give me the effect I want. I try not to get hung up on a stitch that I think will be 'the one' to give me the end product. It usually isn't the right one. "

▲ **Solomon's Knot Bracelet** | 2006

9 x 3 x ¹⁄₁₆ inches (22.8 x 7.6 x 0.2 cm)
Cylinder seed beads, freshwater pearls;
right-angle weave, brick stitch

Photo by Larry Sanders

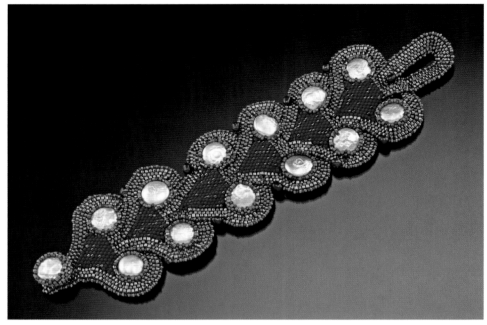

▲ **Mosaic Chain Cuff** | 2006

8½ x 2 x ¹⁄₁₆ inches (21.6 x 5.1 x 0.2 cm)
Cylinder seed beads, freshwater coin
pearls, small freshwater pearls; brick
stitch, peyote stitch

Photo by Larry Sanders

◄ **Scepter Beads** | 2006

1½ inches (3.8 cm)
Cylinder seed beads, gold vermeil
drops, gold-filled ear wires; right-angle
weave, peyote stitch

Photo by Larry Sanders

" I love to combine stitches. It opens up many possibilities for creating my designs. I tell beaders that if you know at least five basic stitches in all of their forms—tubular, circular, flat, etc.—you can begin to develop your own style and have the tools to implement your ideas. The five stitches I recommend are peyote, brick, right-angle weave, herringbone, and square. "

▲ **Byzantine Knot Necklace** | 2005

8 x 9½ x ¼ inches (20.3 x 24.1 x 1.9 cm)
Cylinder seed beads, seed beads, freshwater rice pearls, freshwater pearls; brick stitch, right-angle weave, square stitch
Photo by Larry Sanders

Sharmini Wirasekara

METICULOUS PLANNING and research shape the beautiful work of Sharmini Wirasekara. Her attention to all the details is unsurpassed. The shapes of her finished work always offer more than just straight edges, and her magnificent patterns seem visually layered. The influences of Wirasekara's interest in Mexican history, culture, and architecture abound. In *Aztec*, the bottom edge of the work follows the curves of the pattern, and the robe's sleeves continue the flow of the design seen at the yoke of the garment. Both the front and back of the piece have distinctive designs. Such thoroughness is common to all of Wirasekara's works. She hand graphs each image and uses peyote stitch and cylinder seed beads to express her creative vision. The time and energy taken to graph and stitch these works are daunting, but Wirasekara's love for her craft makes her journey worthwhile—and a thrilling, provocative experience for viewers.

▲ **Tree of Life Necklace** | 2004

17 x 10 inches (43.2 x 25.4 cm)
Cylinder seed beads, round seed beads, leaf-shaped beads, flower-shaped beads; peyote stitch

Photos by Paul vanPeenen

▲ **Aztec** | 2007
13 x 11 x 3 inches (33 x 27.9 x 7.6 cm)
Cylinder seed beads, crystal
beads; peyote stitch
Photos by Barbara Cohen

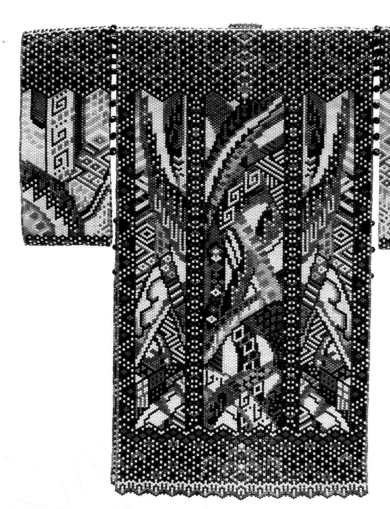

 **Mata Ortiz** | 2007

13½ x 11 x 3 inches (34.3 x 27.9 x 7.6 cm)
Cylinder seed beads, crystal
beads; peyote stitch

Photos by Barbara Cohen

" I moved to Canada from my
native Sri Lanka in 1988,
and gave up a 12-year career
in accounting to immerse
myself in art education.
I enrolled in a textile-art
program at a college and
dabbled in many art forms
and techniques. I specialized
in silk painting for many
years. In 1997 I took a
workshop in off-loom peyote
beadweaving, and I have
been completely addicted to
beading ever since. "

Talavera | 2006 ▶
13 x 11¼ x 3 inches
(33 x 28.6 x 7.6 cm)
Cylinder seed beads,
crystal beads;
peyote stitch
Photo by Barbara Cohen

17 x 10 inches (43.2 x 25.4 cm)
Cylinder seed beads, crystal
beads, antique metallic
ornaments; peyote stitch
Photo by Barbara Cohen

▲ **Lotus** | 2007

13½ x 11 x 3 inches (34.3 x 27.9 x 7.6 cm)
Cylinder seed beads, crystal beads; peyote stitch
Photo by Barbara Cohen

" I use symbolism to bring meaning to each piece. Much research of the subject goes into creating a design. My designs tend to be very intricate and detailed. In some of my work, the designs may look symmetrical at first glance, but on closer inspection the differences, or asymmetrical features, become evident. I feel this creates more interest for the viewer, and therefore it has become a main feature in creating my designs. "

Diego Rivera Necklace | 2004 ▶

15 x 11 inches (38.1 x 27.9 cm)
Cylinder seed beads, round
seed beads, crystal beads; peyote
stitch, right-angle weave

Photo by Paul vanPeenen

▲ **Mexican Tree of History** | 2004

15 x 11 inches (38.1 x 27.9 cm)
Cylinder seed beads, crystal beads,
metallic beads; peyote stitch

Photo by Paul vanPeenen

▲ **Mayan God** | 2003

12 x 8 inches (30.5 x 20.3 cm)
Cylinder seed beads, round seed beads,
metallic hex beads, cord; peyote stitch

Photo by Babara Cohen

" All my designs are hand
drawn, and I don't use
computer programs.
I usually design and
bead a small section at a
time—this allows me to
alter pattern or color as
I go along. My work is
woven horizontally, and
I find it very exciting
to see the pattern take
shape little by little. "

▲ **Mayan Teapot** | 2004
7 x 7 x 1½ inches (17.8 x 17.8 x 1.3 cm)
Cylinder seed beads, metallic beads, foam,
fabric; peyote stitch, right-angle weave
Photo by Barbara Cohen

Laura Leonard

THE MARVELOUS CARICATURES that populate the work of Laura Leonard are revealing, humor-filled looks at life as we all know it. Her three-dimensional beaded figures present all aspects of human nature from Leonard's delightful perspective. Peyote stitch, right-angle weave, and brick stitch are the techniques used to create *Mother-in-Law Cometh*, the arrival of a married couple's worst nightmare embodied in beads. Bright colors and wacky patterns accentuate the ridiculousness of this truthful scenario. How many people can relate to *If the Shoe Fits ... Buy Several?* Are you laughing yet? If you are, catch your breath, and then look at each piece and think about the time and intelligence it has taken to create this unforgettable body of work. Tiny glass beads—added one, two, or three at a time—cover each composition, and knowing when to increase or decrease to shape the figures correctly requires masterful skill and deep patience. Leonard's comic detail and human insight are entrancing. She brings her pieces to vivid life.

▲ **Mother-in-Law Cometh** | 2000
15 x 12 x 8 inches (38.1 x 30.5 x 20.3 cm)
Seed beads, wire, fabric; peyote stitch, right-angle weave, brick stitch
Photo by Petronella Ytsma

▲ **Summer in Fargo** | 2002

  4 x 6 x 6 inches (10.2 x 15.2 x 15.2 cm)
  Seed beads, wire, fabric; peyote stitch

  Photo by Petronella Ytsma

▲ **Baba Yaga: Dedicated to
  the Witch in All of Us** | 2001

  12 x 10 x 7 inches (30.5 x 25.4 x 17.8 cm)
  Seed beads, wire, screen, fabric; peyote stitch,
  brick stitch, square stitch, right-angle weave

  Photo by Petronella Ytsma

◀ **Motorcycle Mama** | 2006

7 x 6 x 6 inches
(17.8 x 15.2 x 15.2 cm)
Seed beads, wire, fabric,
leather, epoxy; peyote stitch

Photo by Petronella Ytsma

" My tagline is 'I make art to feed my soul. I sell art to feed my son.' Humor plays a big role in my work. My first goal when people walk into my booth is to get them laughing. The close second goal is to get them buying so they can help me pay for groceries—the 'feed my son' thing. "

Woman Who Runs with Poodles | 1998

16 x 10 x 7 inches (40.6 x 25.4 x 17.8 cm)
Seed beads, wire, fabric; peyote
stitch, bead embroidery

Photo by Petronella Ytsma

LAURA LEONARD

" I start by making a wire stick figure. This armature is wrapped tightly in fabric—usually strips of old T-shirts. Recently I've been using an epoxy that taxidermists use to build up some facial features and strengthen joints. Then beads—size 11 and 14 seed beads—are sewn together one to three at a time to form a skin that completely covers the armature. "

◀ **Edith Waits** │ 1996

10 x 12 x 12 inches (25.4 x 30.5 x 30.5 cm)
Seed beads, fabric, wire; peyote stitch,
right-angle weave, netting
Photo by Petronella Ytsma

▲ **Martini Sister 2** | 2007

5 x 4 x 2 inches (12.7 x 10.2 x 5.1 cm)
Seed beads, fabric, wire; peyote
stitch, bead embroidery

Photo by Petronella Ytsma

Martini Sister | 2005 ▶

6 x 6 x 4 inches (15.2 x 15.2 x 10.2 cm)
Seed beads, fabric, wire; peyote
stitch, right-angle weave

Photo by Petronella Ytsma

▲ **Twenty-Four Carrot Hare** | 1999

12 x 9 x 8 inches (30.5 x 22.9 x 20.3 cm)
Seed beads, fabric, wire, epoxy; peyote stitch, netting

Photos by Petronella Ytsma

" Winter months are spent beading away while the snow flies and the temps drop. As long as my
eyes hold out (I've got lined trifocals so far) and my wrists are mostly pain-free (I'm wearing
wrist bands for carpal tunnel), I'll be creating beadwork. I'm drawn to quirkiness and the weirder
side of life. No pretty girls here. I often wonder if I'll live long enough to see all of my wacko
creations come to life. "

▲ **If the Shoe Fits . . . Buy Several** │ 1999

    12 x 10 x 8 inches (30.5 x 25.4 x 20.3 cm)
Seed beads, wire, fabric; peyote stitch,
right-angle weave, brick stitch

Photo by artist

▲ **Goddess of Love and Laundry** │ 1996

    14 x 13 x 10 inches (35.6 x 33 x 25.4 cm)
Seed beads, wire, fabric; peyote stitch,
right-angle weave, running stitch,
bead embroidery

Photo by Petronella Ytsma

Leslie Frazier

A FASCINATION WITH three-sided pinch beads led Leslie Frazier to two months of nonstop investigation into the possibilities for their use. Her work gave birth to pieces like *Celestial Necklace* and the beaded-bead components of *Chunky Floral Bead Necklace* and *Woven Beads Lariat*. This last piece includes a combination of herringbone, peyote, and right-angle weave, exemplifying Frazier's inventiveness and ambition. Frazier is willing to experiment, and she's open to happy accident. When herringbone stitch became the beneficiary of her attention, refined work like the oak leaf shapes in *Autumn Glory Necklace* resulted; Frazier gives Mother Nature a run for her money in this stunning necklace. Frazier is a master crafter who takes ideas and explores all the avenues of expression for their best possible artistic effect.

Spring Dreams Lariat | 2003 ▶

Lariat, 26 inches (66 cm) long;
flower diameter, 2⅝ inches (6.7 cm);
leaves, 2½ x ¾ inches (2.5 x 1.9 cm) each
Seed beads, cylinder beads, crystals; spiraling three-dimensional tubular herringbone stitch, decreasing combined tubular herringbone stitch and peyote stitch, flat herringbone stitch

Photo by Tom Frazier

Autumn Glory Necklace | 2007 ▶

Necklace, 20 inches (50.8 cm) long;
center motif, 3½ x 3¼ inches (8.9 x 8.3 cm)
Seed beads, cylinder beads, faceted glass
beads; spiraling tubular herringbone variation,
flat herringbone stitch, peyote stitch, square stitch,
four- and five-bead right-angle stitch, stringing

Photo by Tom Frazier

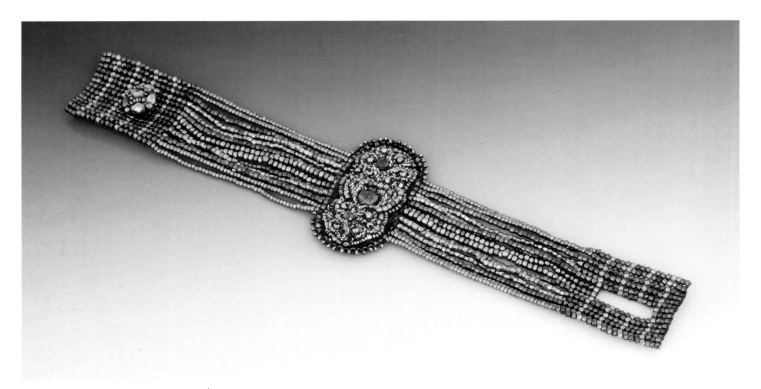

▲ **Victorian Strand Bracelet** | 2003

7½ x 1 inches (19.1 x 2.5 cm);
center motif, 1 x 1⅞ inches (2.5 x 4.7 cm)
Seed beads, cylinder seed beads, vintage nailhead beads,
faceted glass beads, charlotte seed beads, three-cut seed
beads, leather, fabric trim; herringbone stitch, stringing,
embroidery, three-bead edging, woven bead button

Photo by Tom Frazier

" When I was seven years old and complained of being
bored, my mother gave me a little apple-green glass
box. In it, she had stored fragments of broken jewelry.
My boredom melted away and a fascination with
beads took its place. Over the years I've come back to
beads again and again. With beads and a needle and
thread, I'm never wondering what to do. I just start
weaving, and things begin to happen. "

◀ **Gay '90s Necklace** │ 1998

22 inches (55.9 cm) long
Seed beads, cylinder seed beads,
faceted glass beads, crystals, glass
flask, cork, French wire, sterling
silver toggle clasp; tubular peyote
stitch, stringing, fringing, carving

Photos by Tom Frazier

" My goal is that my designs have an immediate impact, and that, as they are viewed more closely, interesting little details, subtle color blends, and fine workmanship give both wearer and viewer continued appreciation. "

◄ **Double Flower Lariat** | 2003
Lariat, 26 inches (66 cm) long;
flowers, 2½ inches (6.3 cm) each in diameter
Seed beads, cylinder seed beads, crystals; spiraling
three-dimensional tubular herringbone stitch, combined
tubular herringbone stitch and peyote stitch, fringing
Photo by Tom Frazier

◀ **Celestial Necklace** | 2006

Necklace, 20 inches (50.8 cm) long;
center motif, 2 x 3 inches (5.1 x 7.6 cm)
Faceted glass beads, pinch beads, seed
beads, crystal beads, sterling silver clasp;
original weave, embellishment

Photos by Tom Frazier

LESLIE FRAZIER

▲ **Estrellita Necklace** │ 2006

Necklace, 20 inches (50.8 cm) long;
star motif, 1½ x 1½ inches (3.8 x 3.8 cm)
Seed beads, crystals, French wire,
sterling silver clasp; netting

Photo by Tom Frazier

▲ **Chunky Floral Bead Necklace** │ 2006

Largest bead, 1¼ x 1 inches (3.2 x 2.5 cm)
Faceted glass beads, pinch beads, seed beads,
crystals, French wire, sterling silver clasp;
original weave, embellishment, stringing

Photo by Tom Frazier

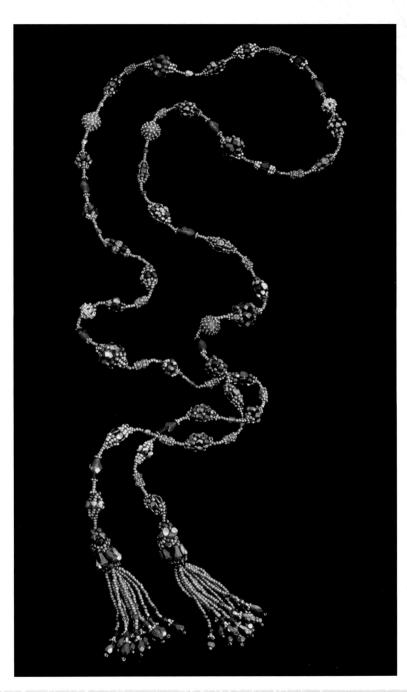

" Beadworkers today are privileged to live in an era with an amazing availability of beads from all parts of the world—old beads, new beads, new shapes, new colors, new finishes. So many possibilities are open to us. After I learned basic brick stitch, square stitch, right-angle weave, peyote stitch, and Ndebele, or herringbone, stitch, I started experimenting, combining differently shaped beads to create woven beads. Weaving my own components to use in a variety of ways has been the main direction of my work. "

◀ **Woven Beads Lariat** | 2001

55 inches (139.7 cm) long
Faceted glass beads, pinch beads, seed beads, crystals, sterling silver beads and spacers; herringbone stitch, peyote stitch, right-angle weave, stringing, fringing
Photo by Tom Frazier

Don Pierce

WHAT ARE THE LIMITS of loom beadweaving? Perhaps we'll never know, because Don Pierce always finds ways to expand them out a bit further. In each work he tries something new. The shapes of his pieces are interesting from all points of view. Pierce is constantly inventing new surface textures and creative graphic designs. He folds, layers, and fringes; his work is never visually flat. *School of Fishes* uses the fins of the fish to create protruding texture along the piece's outside edges. He also employs both interrupted and supplemental warps to create open spaces throughout the work. *Golden Drape* has three layers of wonderful folded fringe, and Pierce uses beads on the warp threads to generate interest along the piece's straps. Although physically flat, *Tumbling Blocks* packs a three-dimensional punch with its cascading design and use of color. Pierce's work is all about precision, experimentation, and versatility within the supposed confines of beading on a loom.

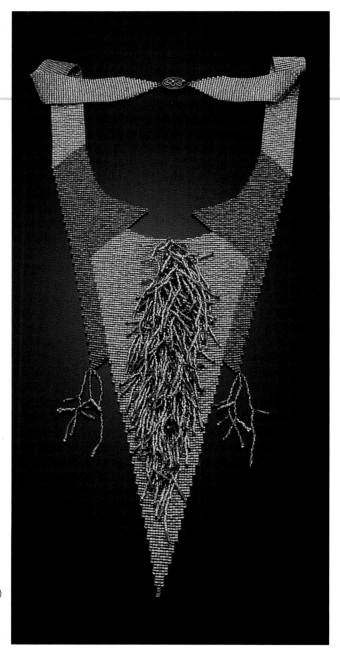

Hairy Chest | 1997 ▶

18 x 6 inches (45.7 x 15.2 cm)
Cylinder seed beads; loom
woven, branched fringe

Photo by Martin Kilmer

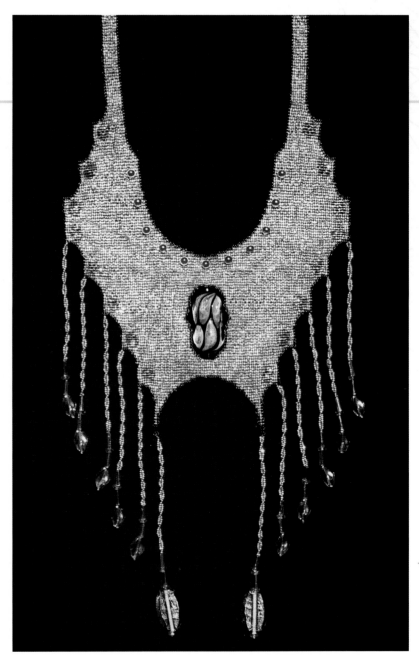

◀ **Golden Butterfly** | 2001

16 x 6 inches (40.6 x 15.2 cm)
24-karat gold-lined Czech seed
beads, metallic charlottes, center
bead by Tom Boylen; loom woven

Photo by Martin Kilmer

▲ **Shaman #1** | 2000

6 x 12 inches (15.2 x 30.5 cm)
Cylinder seed beads, vintage beads, large
bead by Olive Glass, deer hair, feathers,
pine nuts, fiber cord; loom woven, folded

Photo by Martin Kilmer

▲ **Self Portrait** | 2001

3 x 4 inches (7.6 x 10.2 cm)
Cylinder seed beads, Czech glass beads, fiber
cord, brass tube; loom woven, folded, sewn

Photo by Martin Kilmer

" I was inspired to try loom weaving after seeing work by Virginia Blakelock in early

1987. I purchased her book *Those Bad Bad Beads* and started. I have been challenged

to push the envelope with new techniques or variations of old ones and enjoy the tests

of the what-ifs and how-tos. "

▲ **Tumbling Blocks** | 1989

6¼ x 23 inches (15.9 x 58.4 cm)
Cylinder seed beads; loom woven

Photo by Martin Kilmer

Golden Drape | 1996 ▶

6 x 18 inches (15.2 x 45.7 cm)
Cylinder seed beads, antique silk
and wood beads; loom woven

Photo by Martin Kilmer

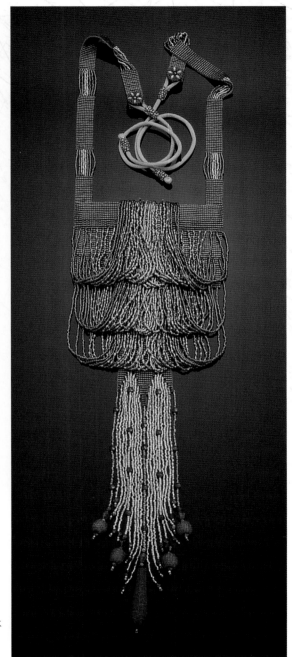

" The bead loom Larry the Loom Mark IV is my design, and it is very versatile and easy to use. Larry has been shipped to every continent but Antarctica. Does anyone know a bead person in Antarctica? "

——————————

Shimmy and Shake │ 1988 ▶

6 x 18 inches (15.2 x 45.7 cm)
Czech cut beads, copper
tubes; loom woven
Photo by Jim Thornton

DON PIERCE

164

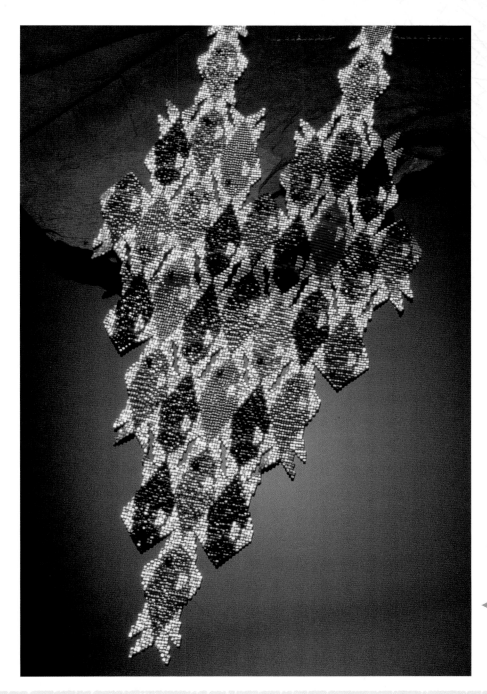

◀ **School of Fishes** │ 1997

    21 x 8 inches (53.3 x 20.3 cm)
Cylinder seed beads, antique
nailheads; loom woven, appliquéd

Photo by Martin Kilmer

▲ **Evening Bag** | 2004

6 x 9 inches (15.2 x 22.9 cm)
Aiko beads, satin lining,
braided cord strap;
loom woven

Photo by Martin Kilmer

◀ **Art Deco #7** | 2002

6 x 18 inches (15.2 x 45.7 cm)
Aiko beads; loom woven

Photo by artist

Seminole Quilt | 1998

8 x 16 inches (20.3 x 40.6 cm)
Czech satin beads; loom woven
Photo by Martin Kilmer

" I have enjoyed teaching and traveling all over the country, but lately I've curtailed my teaching, as I have enough hotel soap to last the rest of my life. "

Laura McCabe

LUSH, TACTILE, VINTAGE, and sometimes unnerving, Laura McCabe's beadwork flows from her mind to her hand with organic precision. Every surface is embellished, and every piece glows with the richness of her excellent technique. McCabe combines her knowledge about historical costumes, textiles, and cultures with diverse beading techniques. The necklace *Infinity* is fit for a queen and, in fact, uses McCabe's hollow form *Crown Jewels* as part of its components. The complex centerpiece features an unforgettable beaded bead within a bead. McCabe is inventive and not bound by conformity. She lets her little girl out and shows viewers that glitter and sparkle are good for the spirit and soul. Humor is beneficial, as well, and McCabe's *The Eyes Have It* both wards off evil spirits and makes viewers laugh at the incongruity of it all. McCabe pushes the limits in expressing her brilliant, decorative vision.

Dahlia | 2002 ▶

28 inches (71.1 cm) long
Green moonstone, Japanese seed beads, Czech and German glass beads, vintage micro beads, freshwater pearls, antique Bakelite buttons, leather, nylon thread; peyote stitch, embroidery, spiral stitch, branch fringe, embellishment

Photo by Joanne Schmaltz

◀ Infinity | 2006

Necklace, 19 inches (48.2 cm) long; center bead, 1¾ x 1¾ x 1¾ inches (4.4 x 4.4 x 4.4 cm)
Japanese and Czech glass seed beads, vintage Swarovski crystal stones, Swarovski crystal bicones, freshwater pearls, Fireline beading thread; peyote stitch, hollow form construction, spiral stitch, branch fringe, embellishment

Photos by Melinda Holden

" My first experiences with beads were as a young child playing with my great, great aunt's 'pop beads' and 1950s costume jewelry. I knew from the very beginning that it was my calling. In college, I studied historical costume restoration and reproduction and specialized in the beaded garments of the Victorian era and the 1920s. "

◄ **Cyclops** | 2002

Necklace, 18 inches (45.7 cm) long; eye, 1¼ inches (3.2 cm)
Glass alligator eye, Japanese and Czech glass seed beads, Czech and German glass beads, freshwater pearls, nylon thread; peyote stitch, embroidery, spiral stitch, branch fringe, embellishment
Photo by Melinda Holden

▲ **Crown Jewels** | 2005

1¾ x 1¾ inches (4.4 x 4.4 cm)
Japanese and Czech glass seed beads, vintage
Swarovski crystal stones, Swarovski-crystal
bicones, Fireline beading thread; peyote
stitch, hollow form construction

Photo by Melinda Holden

◀ **Pokeweed Berry Lariat Necklace** | 2003

Necklace, 30 inches (76.2 cm) long;
berry clusters, 3-4 inches (7-10 cm) each
Japanese glass seed beads, freshwater pearls,
green moonstone cabochon, German glass
flowers, Chinese opaline glass beads, antique
steel cut beads, leather; embroidery, peyote
stitch, spiral stitch, embellishment

Photo by Robert Liu

▲ **The Eyes Have It** | 2004

Necklace, 20 inches (50. 8 cm) long;
eyes, 1 x 1 inches (2.5 x 2.5 cm) each
Antique prosthetic glass eyes, Japanese glass
seed beads, vintage steel cut beads, vintage
Czech glass seed beads, Czech and Chinese glass
beads, freshwater pearls, leather, nylon thread;
embroidery, peyote stitch, embellishment

Photos by Melinda Holden

" Beads and beadwork have a universal
appeal that links people across cultures
and ages. Beads date back more than
40,000 years, and they are a uniquely
human phenomena, not found amongst
other primates or even earlier human
species. In addition to serving the human
needs of vanity, adornment, and social
status, beads have a deeper, more spiritual
aspect: They provide good fortune,
protection from evil forces, and links to a
more spiritual realm. "

▲ Elfin Armour Beaded Collar | 2003

10 x 12 inches (25.4 x 30.5 cm)
Japanese glass seed beads, opalized fossil clam,
pearlized fossil ammonite, pyratized fossil
ammonite, abalone, coin pearls, opal rondelles,
freshwater pearls, leather, suede, nylon thread;
embroidery, peyote stitch, embellishment

Photo by Joanne Schmaltz

▼ Keshi Pearl Necklace | 2005

17 inches (43.2 cm) long
Japanese glass seed beads, keshi pearls,
freshwater pearls, German glass flowers,
enameled copper button, nylon thread;
spiral stitch, peyote stitch, embellishment

Photo by Melinda Holden

" By drawing on my education in historical costumes and textiles and applying variations of Native American, African Zulu, and Victorian beading techniques to contemporary colors and designs, I strive to create beaded body adornment that celebrates and reincarnates the dying tradition of fine handcrafts. "

Common Thread | 2004 ▶

Necklace, 20 inches (50 cm) long;
center front piece, 3 x 1 inches (7.6 x 2.5 cm)
Japanese and Czech glass beads, vintage
Italian micro beads, vintage Swarovski
rivoli stone, German glass flowers, vintage
rose montees, cubic zirconia beads, antique
micro button, Fireline beading thread;
herringbone stitch, peyote stitch, lacy
stitch, embellishment

Photo by Melinda Holden

LAURA McCABE

Peacock Headpiece | 2005 ▶

Front piece, 2 x 2 inches (5.1 x 5.1 cm)
Antique pressed glass cabochon, Japanese and
Czech glass seed beads, crystal beads, crystal
stones, crystal sequins, Fireline beading
thread, leather, nylon thread; embroidery,
peyote stitch, embellishment

Photos by Joanne Schmaltz

Madelyn C. Ricks

FROM ART DECO DESIGNS to bursting, bright patterns to the serenity of a kimono, the work of Madelyn C. Ricks has evolved in as thought-provoking a manner as the precise patterns she designs. Ricks' earlier works include joyful explosions of color. Myriad designs move all around *Vessel with Stand* with a cohesiveness created by a limited palette. Peyote, Ricks' stitch of choice, moves from flat to dimensional in *Mardi Gras Teapot*, a vivacious testament to her sense of fun. *Kimono, Jewel Colors* was one of Ricks' first steps toward her newer works, a combination of bright patterning with the kimono form. As she stitches these flowing garments, a Japanese sensibility seems to influence the designs. Ricks first graphs the designs and then meticulously chooses each cylinder, brilliantly exhibiting what careful planning and creative thought can do when put together in her inspiring beadwork.

Kimono, Jewel Colors | 2000 ▶

11 x 9 x 1 inches (27.9 x 22.9 x 2.5 cm)
Cylinder seed beads; peyote stitch

Photo by Jerry Anthony

◀ **E-R Orchids Kimono** | 2007

21 x 16 x 1 inches (53.3 x 40.6 x 2.5 cm)
Cylinder seed beads; peyote stitch
Photos by Catherine Kalomu

" I've always felt I was meant to have lived in an earlier time. One of the reasons I'm so drawn to beading is that there are no machines and no fancy equipment—just needle, thread, beads, and time. I find the slow, deliberate rhythm of creating beadwork very comforting. Seeing patterns develop slowly, and small patterns turn into larger ones, is very gratifying to me. "

Purple Iris Kimono | 2006 ▶

21 x 16 x 1 inches
(53.3 x 40.6 x 2.5 cm)
Cylinder seed beads;
peyote stitch

Photos by Catherine Kalomu

▼ Peacock Kimono | 2007

21 x 16 x 1 inches (53.3 x 40.6 x 2.5 cm)
Cylinder seed beads; peyote stitch

Photos by Catherine Kalomu

" I've never felt the need to create pieces that made some deep statement about the social problems of our time or that were very thought provoking. My main goal has always been to make work that brings a sense of joy and, hopefully, beauty to viewers. I love it when people tell me that my work makes them smile. "

Cherry Blossoms on Red | 2006 ▶
  14 x 12 x 1 inches (35.6 x 30.5 x 2.5 cm)
  Cylinder seed beads; peyote stitch
  Photos by Jerry Anthony

Feathers Kimono | 2005 ▶

12 x 9 x 1 inches (30.5 x 22.9 x 2.5 cm)
Cylinder seed beads; peyote stitch

Photo by Jerry Anthony

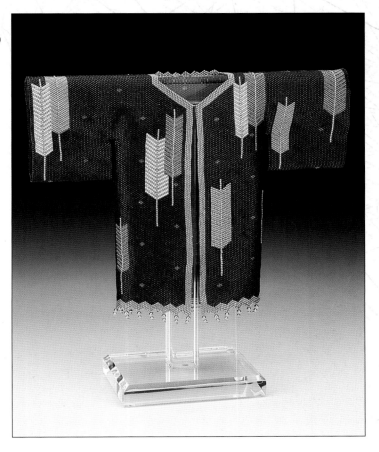

◀ **Brocade Wedding Kimono** | 2005

12 x 12 x 1 inches (30.5 x 30.5 x 2.5 cm)
Cylinder seed beads; peyote stitch

Photo by Jerry Anthony

" I worked full time as a ceramic artist for more than 16 years. As I passed my mid-fifties, I realized I had to change what I was doing. My works in clay were getting bigger, and I was getting older. I definitely needed to scale down. More than 10 years later, I'm so addicted to beading that I'm at a total loss when I've finished a piece and haven't yet finalized the next design, so I can start beading a new piece. "

Mardi Gras Teapot | 2002 ▶
14 x 4 x 6 inches
(35.6 x 10.2 x 15.2 cm)
Cylinder seed beads, plastic
tubing, wire; peyote stitch
Photo by Jerry Anthony

▲ Coil Wrap Neckpiece | 2000
16 x 13 x 2 inches (40.6 x 33 x 5.1 cm)
Cylinder seed beads, plastic tubing,
spring wire; peyote stitch
Photo by Jerry Anthony

▲ **Late Bloomer** | 1999

14 x 11 x 6 inches (35.6 x 27.9 x 15.2 cm)
Cylinder seed beads, plastic
tubing, wire; peyote stitch

Photo by Jerry Anthony

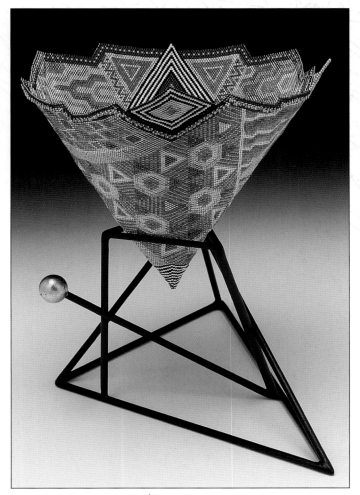

▲ **Vessel with Stand** | 1999

10 x 8 x 8 inches (25.4 x 20.3 x 20.3 cm)
Cylinder seed beads, wood, polychrome,
gold leaf; peyote stitch

Photo by Larry Sanders

Melanie Potter

A NEW AND ENERGETIC WEAVER in the bead world, Melanie Potter designs sleek, contemporary, wearable art. Potter is proficient in many off-loom stitches and uses them to outstanding effect in her work. She loves engineering projects. Deciding which stitch to use where, which bead size is best, and how to put it all together so the piece hangs properly—all contribute to her thought process. Yet she remains open and fluid as she does the work, willing to make whatever changes are necessary to achieve the results of her original creative vision. This inner drive to keep making forward progress until the work is just right is the sign of a true craftsperson. The end result? Potter's spectacular work is clean, precise, feminine, and definitely wearable.

Plaid Dominoes | 2004 ▶

1⅜ x ¼ x 6½ inches (3.5 x 0.6 x 16.5 cm)
Seed beads, crystals, thread, paper clip;
right-angle weave, peyote stitch,
chevron chain stitch

Photo by Scott Potter

◀ **Swag Collar** | 2007

⅛ x 1¹⁄₁₆ x 16 inches
(0.3 x 4.6 x 40.6 cm)
Seed beads, crystal
stones, thread;
chevron chain stitch,
peyote stitch,
herringbone stitch
Photo by Scott Potter

▲ **Circular Chevron Lace Beads** | 2003

½ x ½ x 19 inches (1.3 x 1.3 x 48.3 cm)
Seed beads, crystal spacers, faceted stones, gold clasp and
findings, wire, thread; circular chevron chain stitch, stringing
Photo by Scott Potter

" Beading has three main aspects that provide a nice variety of activity: designing the piece and pattern; creating color palettes; and beading samples. Designing requires an approach that is methodical and well thought out. Selecting bead colors for each palette combination is a very calming, contemplative experience. Beading samples for hours on end requires an immovable endurance of purpose—a determination that bears great fruit once the work is completed. "

String Quartet Collar | 2005

⅟₁₆ x 1½ x 14 inches (0.2 x 3.8 x 35.6 cm)
Crystals, seed beads, gold findings,
thread; right-angle weave, netting

Photo by Scott Potter

Lunar Lights | 2006 ▶

1¹⁄₁₆ x ¼ x 6½ inches (3.7 x 0.6 x 16.5 cm)
Seed beads, crystals, thread, nylon snap;
right-angle weave, peyote stitch, chevron
chain stitch, three-bead picots

Photo by Scott Potter

◀ **Ribbonesque** | 2006

4½ x 3¼ x ½ inches (11.4 x 8.3 x 1.3 cm)
Seed beads, crystals, thread, tie tack pin; peyote
stitch, netting, square stitch, right-angle weave
Photo by Scott Potter

" I wear each jewelry piece to see if it is comfortable and wearable. If not, it goes back into the development phase to figure out how to get it there. I absolutely love wearing the things I design. These pieces are expressions of shapes and colors that I think are beautiful and wearable. I also love glitter. Even as a child I gravitated toward all things that glittered, and I had no qualms wearing glitter morning, noon, or night. In my mind, it was good for any occasion—and it still is! "

◀ **Ribbon of Notre Dame** | 2005

⅛ x ¾ x 38 inches (0.3 x 1.9 x 96.5 cm)
Seed beads, thread;
right-angle weave, netting
Photo by Scott Potter

▲ **Crystal Swag** | 2006

¼ x ¾ x 16 inches (0.6 x 1.9 x 40.6 cm)
Seed beads, crystals, thread; chevron chain stitch,
circular chevron chain stitch, herringbone stitch,
peyote stitch, right-angle weave

Photo by Scott Potter

Resplendent Pendant Earrings | 2007

1½ x ¼ x ⅜ inches (3.8 x 0.6 x 1 cm)
Seed beads, crystal stones, sterling silver posts;
right-angle weave, circular chevron chain
stitch, peyote stitch, herringbone stitch

Photo by Scott Potter

Crystal Plume Earrings | 2007 ▶

⅝ x 1¾ x ⅜ inches (1.5 x 4.4 x 1 cm)
Seed beads, crystal briolettes, crystal
stone, sterling silver posts; right-angle
weave, circular chevron chain stitch,
peyote stitch, herringbone stitch

Photo by Scott Potter

" I was introduced to off-loom seed-bead weaving in 1999 through my daughter Christina's interest in it. When I saw the things she was beading, I was enamored, and felt compelled to try it out. I had a strong knowledge of couture sewing, and this knowledge transferred easily to beading. Christina has a very high expectation for quality in the pieces I create. If something I bead seems unfinished to her, she lets me know in a very kind way that motivates me to push harder for a better outcome. "

▲ **Egyptian Lotus Lariat** | 2004
¼ x ¼ x 32 inches (0.6 x 0.6 x 81.3 cm)
Seed beads, crystals, thread; circular chevron chain stitch, two-drop peyote stitch, three-bead picots
Photo by Scott Potter

Huib Petersen

TAKING AN EXHILARATING PATH through nature's themes and wonders, Huib Petersen uses a variety of stitches to interpret a multitude of living creatures and their habitats. He distills the overall view of a garden down to its smallest occupants—the insects—and their communion with flowers or their connection with each other. Each Petersen necklace tells its own story, from the complexity of nesting birds presented in *Fall in Love* to the simplicity of flowers creating a *Daisy Chain*. In *Monarch Migration*, his grouping of orange and black butterflies created with peyote stitch takes viewers to Mexico to see the creatures' seasonal flight. The ocean and its inhabitants draw Petersen's attention in *Neckquarium* and *Ocean Bottom*—even the jellyfish look good in his delightful renditions. Petersen's excitement about beadwork and life comes through in his vibrant and vital depictions of the natural world.

The Gathering | 2006 ▶

16 x 9 x 1 inches (40.6 x 22.9 x 2.5 cm)
Seed beads, pearls, semiprecious stones; diagonal peyote stitch, tubular peyote stitch

Photo by artist

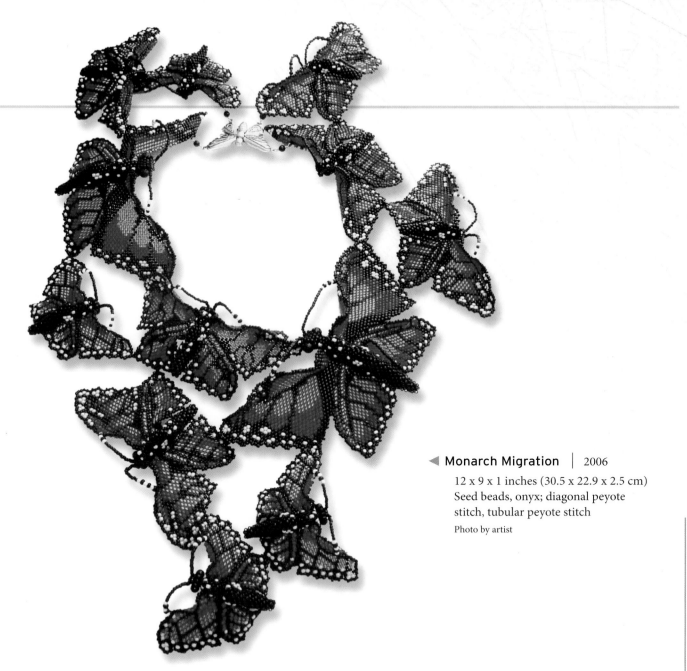

◀ **Monarch Migration** | 2006

12 x 9 x 1 inches (30.5 x 22.9 x 2.5 cm)
Seed beads, onyx; diagonal peyote
stitch, tubular peyote stitch

Photo by artist

" I think a thought or idea starts in our experiences through our senses: taste, smell, sight, sound, and touch. This is where my inspiration, insight, knowledge, and clarity come from: my experiences with the world and the people who surround me. "

▲ **Ocean Bottom** | 2004

Necklace, 16 inches (40 cm) long;
big starfish, 3½ x 3½ x 1 inches (8.9 x 8.9 x 2.5 cm)
Seed beads; tubular peyote stitch,
circular peyote stitch

Photo by artist

▲ **Neckquarium** | 2001

Necklace, 16 inches (40 cm) long;
fish, 1½ x 1 x 1 inches (3.8 x 2.5 x 2.5 cm) each
Seed beads, pearls, shells; tubular
peyote stitch, embellishment

Photo by artist

▲ **Fall in Love** | 2003

Necklace, 17 inches (41 cm) long;
birds, 3 x 2½ x 1 inches (7.6 x 6.4 x 2.5 cm) each;
nest, 1½ x 1 x 2½ inches (3.8 x 2.5 x 6.4 cm)
Seed beads, pearls; tubular peyote stitch,
diagonal peyote stitch, herringbone stitch

Photo by artist

▲ **Resting in Ivy** | 1998

Necklace, 16 inches (40 cm) long;
butterflies, 8 x 10 x 1 inches (20.3 x 25.4 x 2.5 cm) each
Seed beads, onyx; diagonal peyote stitch,
tubular peyote stitch, herringbone stitch

Photo by artist

▲ **Daisy Chain** | 2003

Flowers, ¾ x ¾ x ½ inches (1.9 x 1.9 x 1.3 cm) each;
stems, 2½ inches (6.4 cm) each
Seed beads; tubular peyote stitch,
herringbone stitch, embellishment

Photo by artist

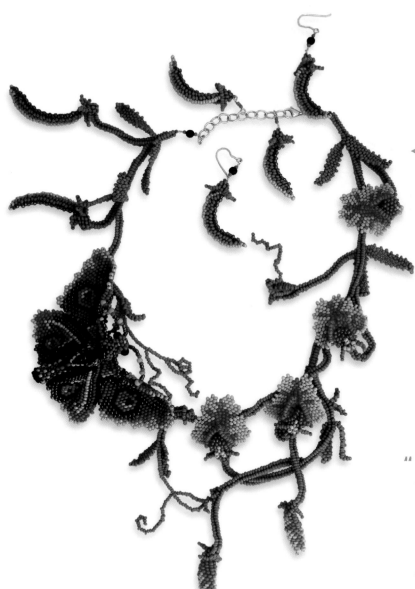

◀ **Wild Pea Butterfly** | 2002

Necklace, 16 inches (40 cm) long;
butterfly, 6 x 10 x 1 inches (15.2 x 25.4 x 2.5 cm)
Seed beads, pearls, crystals; diagonal peyote
stitch, tubular peyote stitch, herringbone stitch

Photo by artist

" My father is a mason. What I do in my

beadwork is like what my father does

in miniature. My beads are the stones,

my thread the mortar. "

HUIB **PETERSEN**

197

Waiting for Prey | 2005 ▶

Necklace, 16 inches (40 cm) long;
spider, 9 x 7 x 1 inches (22.9 x 17.8 x 2.5 cm)
Seed beads, amethyst; diagonal peyote stitch,
tubular peyote stitch, embellishment

Photos by artist

" Beadwork seems to me to be a combination of all the skills I've learned in my life. It combines embroidery, crochet, knitting, bobbin lace, sculpting, and painting. I like the wearable aspect of beadwork, the reflection of light, and the movement and joy of the wearer, which bring my pieces more to life. "

◀ **Summer Serenade** │ 2005

Necklace, 16 inches (40 cm) long;
cricket, 1 x 1½ x ½ inches (2.5 x 3.8 x 1.3 cm)
Seed beads, amethyst; diagonal peyote stitch,
tubular peyote stitch

Photos by artist

Sherry Serafini

INVENTIVE CRAFTSMANSHIP SETS APART the purses, collars, and bracelets of Sherry Serafini. Her designs are strong and original, and most of her pieces feature both peyote stitch and freeform bead embroidery. From dyeing the foundation material to sewing on the backing, each step is done with the utmost care. Serafini's meticulousness and her design wisdom are seen in her basic shapes, placement of focal beads, and choices of bead color. The triangular form of *Genie's New Hangout* is anchored by symmetrically centered focal beads, while asymmetrical secondary cabochons and crystals pull the eye around the purse. As the main crystal draws viewers into the piece's depths, varied embellishment beads keep attention on the front surface and bring the seed beads to light. Serafini's color and placement choices are integral to each work. Combining beadweaving and bead embroidery, Sherry Serafini takes both art forms to another level.

Night on the Town | 2004 ▶

8 x 6½ x 3 inches (20.3 x 16.5 x 7.6 cm)
Seed beads, vintage glass, crystals,
bugle beads, assorted beads, pearls,
cabochons; bead embroidery,
peyote stitch, embellishment
Photo by Larry Sanders

Mermaid's Attire | 2006 ▶

12 x 6½ inches (30.5 x 16.5 cm)
Seed beads, turquoise, crystals,
cabochons; bead embroidery,
peyote stitch, embellishment, fringe

Photos by Larry Sanders

◀ **Genie's New Hangout** | 2005

8 x 5 x 5 inches (20.3 x 12.7 x 12.7 cm)
Seed beads, assorted beads, crystals, cabochons; bead embroidery, peyote stitch, embellishment, brick stitch, spiral stitch

Photos by Larry Sanders

" My grandmother was one of my biggest influences in life. She was a feisty little red-haired woman who wore tons of jewelry, even if she was just hanging out at home. She had incredible style. She let me rummage through her jewelry boxes and take broken jewelry to play with. When I discovered the art of beading, I realized I was drawing from my memories of her elaborate jewelry boxes. "

◀ **Hidden Treasure** | 2006

8 x 6 x 4 inches (20.3 x 15.2 x 10.2 cm)
Seed beads, mother-of-pearl, abalone,
ammonite, freshwater pearls, crystals;
bead embroidery, peyote stitch,
embellishment, fringe

Photo by Larry Sanders

" Inspiration is everywhere. I can find a reason to start a new design by listening to a great song by my favorite band, walking in the woods with my dogs, or seeing a vintage piece of jewelry. I have a library of books that I visit for inspiration, covering everything from Egyptian history to the jewels of Miriam Haskell. Shapes also send my mind whirling into a creative frenzy. "

The Gift | 2007 ▶

23 x 8 inches (58.4 x 20.3 cm)
Seed beads, vintage buttons, crystals, cabochons; bead embroidery, peyote stitch, embellishment, fringe
Photo by Larry Sanders

SHERRY SERAFINI

▲ Nicole │ 2002

　　18 x 7½ inches (45.7 x 19.1 cm)
　　Seed beads, crystals, cabochons; bead
　　embroidery, peyote stitch, fringe

　　Photo by Larry Sanders

▲ Seasons of Wither │ 2003

　　12 x 6 inches (30.5 x 15.2 cm)
　　Seed beads, patina metal drops, crystals,
　　cabochons; bead embroidery, peyote stitch,
　　embellishment, brick stitch, fringe

　　Photo by Larry Sanders

" I believe that all gifts are given to us by God and most certainly meant to be shared with each other. There can never be enough beauty in this world. My hopes are that my work inspires others to want to create and find the peace that I find when I sit down to work with my beads. "

Million Dollar Baby | 2007 ▶

24 x 10½ inches (61 x 26.7 cm)
Seed beads, vintage crystals, cabochons; bead embroidery, peyote stitch, right-angle weave, embellishment, fringe
Photos by Larry Sanders

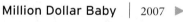

▲ **My Gothic Side** │ 2006

5 x 9 x 3 inches
(12.7 x 22.9 x 7.6 cm)
Seed beads, crystals,
cabochons;
bead embroidery,
peyote stitch

Photos by Larry Sanders

◄ **Crystal Eyes** │ 2004

9 x 6 inches (22.9 x 15.2 cm)
Seed beads, vintage crystals, freshwater pearls,
crystals, cabochons; bead embroidery, freeform
peyote stitch, embellishment, fringe

Photo by Larry Sanders

Wendy Ellsworth

DIVE DOWN INTO THE DEPTHS OF THE SEA and encounter the myriad seaforms birthed in the bright imagination of the Rev. Wendy Ellsworth. Capturing the essence of what's below the surface—literally and figuratively—is one of Ellsworth's many talents. In her *SeaForm* series, freeform peyote stitch and herringbone stitch create designs with a degree of inventive realism. Each layered ruffle and contrasting color draws the eye deeper into the work. The complexity of the shapes, formed by increasing and decreasing stitches, is a marvel. I can just see the seaforms slowly making their way across the bottom of the ocean, or flowing back and forth with the movement of the water. When she ventures above ground, Ellsworth's sense of nature is equally well developed. In *Fall Splendor*, a snake rustles as the leaves and weather turn crisp. Ellsworth wraps up viewers' senses and attention in beaded wonders.

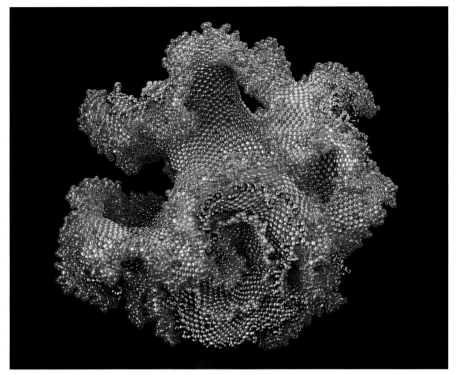

▲ **Maui Seaform** | 1996
3½ x 4½ x 4½ inches (8.9 x 11.4 x 11.4 cm)
Seed beads; freeform gourd stitch, multi-layered
Photo by David Ellsworth

▲ **Fiesta Seaform** | 1995

3¼ x 4 x 4 inches (8.3 x 10.2 x 10.2 cm)
Seed beads; freeform gourd stitch, multi-layered

Photo by David Ellsworth

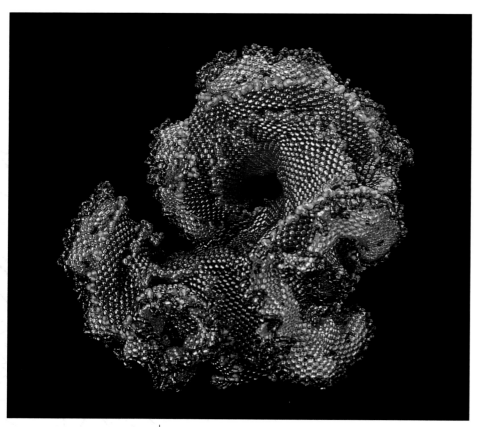

" My love affair with seed
beads began in 1970, just after
graduating from the University
of Colorado. I was living in a
single-room log cabin at 10,500
feet in the Rocky Mountains
with no running water or
electricity, and I began beading
by the light of kerosene lamps.
I beaded circular mandalas in
geometric patterns that were
laced onto leather handbags I
taught myself how to make. "

▲ **Montserrat Seaform** | 1996
  4 x 5 x 5 inches (10.2 x 12.7 x 12.7 cm)
  Seed beads; freeform gourd stitch, multi-layered
  Photo by David Ellsworth

▲ **Blue Seaform** | 1995

3 x 5½ x 5½ inches (7.6 x 13.2 x 13.2 cm)
Seed beads; free-form gourd stitch, multi-layered
Photo by David Ellsworth

◀ **Cancun Seaform** │ 1995

4½ x 5 x 5 inches (11.4 x 12.7 x 12.7 cm)
Seed beads, blown and etched
glass base; freeform gourd
stitch, multi-layered

Photo by David Ellsworth

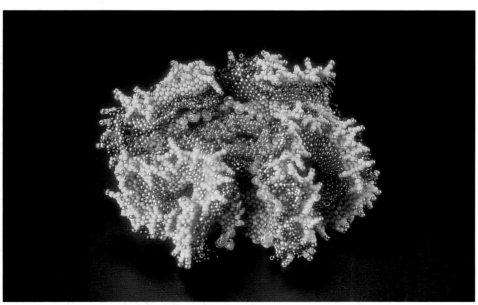

◀ **Selat Siberut Seaform** │ 1997

2½ x 4 x 4 inches (6.4 x 10.2 x 10.2 cm)
Seed beads; freeform gourd
stitch, multi-layered

Photo by David Ellsworth

" As I create my *SeaForm* series, I remember what it felt like to snorkel in the ocean at the Great Barrier Reef off the Australian coast. I was filled with awe at watching the sunlight pass through the water and shine on the coral reef and multitudes of diaphanous fish. The forms, textures, and colors of this living ecosystem gave me a lifetime of inspiration. I find coral reefs incredibly sensual, fluid like the element they live in, elegant, and sometimes comical. "

▲ **Selat Bangka Seaform** | 2002

6 x 5 x 4 inches (15.2 x 12.7 x 10.2 cm)
Seed beads, dagger beads, lentil beads;
freeform gourd stitch, herringbone stitch

Photo by David Ellsworth

▲ **Fall Splendor** | 2001

31 x 11½ x 2 inches (78.7 x 29.2 x 5.1 cm)
Seed beads, wool roving, turned wooden acorns;
tubular herringbone stitch, freeform herringbone stitch

Photos by David Ellsworth

" I have a small studio that sits in the middle of our forest in eastern Pennsylvania, where I work by myself. Color surrounds me and excites me on all levels, and I find inspiration from observing Mother Nature in all her seasonal wardrobes. I consider myself a color artist, with beads representing tiny photons of colored light that can be woven together to form infinite patterns of beauty and delight. "

▲ Earth Fire | 1999

21½ x 6 x 3¾ inches (54.6 x 15.2 x 9.5 cm)
Seed beads, bugles, faceted glass beads, cylinder beads,
dichroic glass button, lampworked beads, Australian opal,
cubes, pinch beads, teardrops, hex beads; freeform gourd stitch
Photo by David Ellsworth

Cynthia Rutledge

TEXTURED SHAPES, multiple techniques, semiprecious beads, and subtle colorations permeate Cynthia Rutledge's work. Her multifaceted designs yield complex, well-conceived works of art. Rutledge is a master at creating interesting and unexpected shapes by moving with ease from one technique to another and back again, repeating and adding variations to expand what can be done with certain stitches. The specifics of the stitches are secondary to achieving the desired effect the finished piece demands. In *Ring Around the Posies* the strap of the necklace could have been left plain and flat—that would have been easy—but Rutledge embellishes the surface with beads, and what a difference the extra work makes. Her use of color builds depth and character in her work, as shown in *Monet Garden Necklace*. The impeccable attention to detail in Rutledge's designs is part and parcel of her creative vision about what will make the work whole and complete.

Ring Around the Posies | 2005 ▶

Necklace, 18 inches (45.7 cm) long;
flowers, 1 x 1 x ½ inches (2.5 x 2.5 x 1.3 cm) each
Seed beads, Czech glass rondelles, snap, suede;
peyote stitch with variation thread path, peyote
stitch, embellishment, split fringe, edge stitching

Photo by Melinda Holden

Turkish Veil | 2007 ▶

36 x 8 x ¼ inches (91.4 x 20.3 x 0.6 cm)
Seed beads, semiprecious beads, pearls,
Czech glass beads, Swarovski crystals,
Bali spacers; lattice weave, herringbone
stitch, peyote stitch, fringe

Photos by Melinda Holden

" I don't dream in color, but I do bead in my dreams. Most of the time, my dream beading is a reflection of how my beadwork has progressed during the day. If there have been design issues, and I have stepped away from the piece, dream beading takes over. It is amazing how well I bead in that state of mind! Most problem areas are worked out during these sessions. "

◀ **Circlet of Lace** | 2006

20 x 1½ x ⅜ inches (50.8 x 3.8 x 1 cm)
Seed beads, pearls, toothpick; peyote
stitch, herringbone stitch, netting,
split circle techniques in peyote
stitch, embellishment

Photo by Melinda Holden

◀ **Chantilly Lace** | 2006

18 x 1½ x 2 inches (45.7 x 3.8 x 5.1 cm)
Seed beads, fire-polished beads, Czech
glass faceted rondelles; herringbone
stitch, peyote stitch, brick stitch

Photo by Melinda Holden

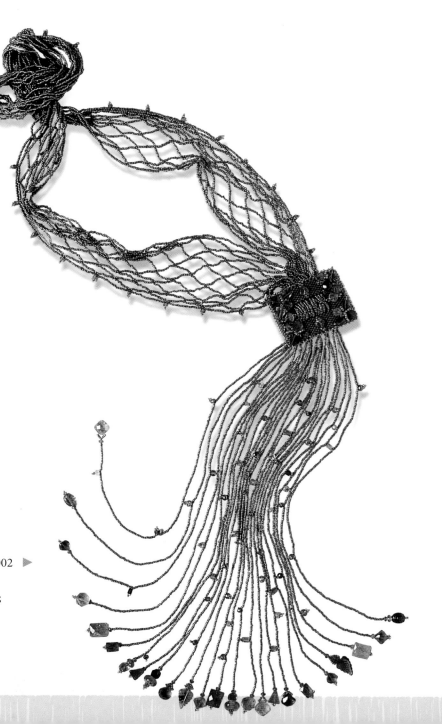

"The choice to use beads as my medium was influenced primarily by my love of color. Beads reflect and absorb light and hold shape and dimension—they offer chameleon-like qualities."

Jeweled Buckle Necklace | 2002 ▶

Necklace, 22 inches (55.8 cm) long; buckle, 1¼ x 2 inches (3.2 x 5.1 cm); fringe, 7 inches (17.8 cm)
Cylinder seed beads, seed beads, semiprecious beads; peyote stitch, vertical netting, fringe

Photos by Melinda Holden

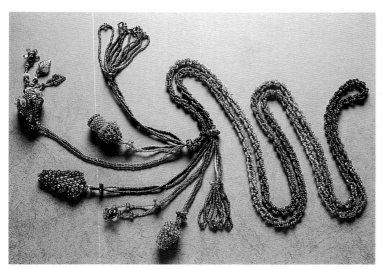

▲ Romancing the Lariat | 1998

62 inches (157.5 cm) long
Seed beads, Czech glass beads, keshi pearls, pearls,
semiprecious beads, Bali spacers, lampworked beads;
peyote stitch, fringe, twisted rope technique

Photos by Melinda Holden

▼ Art Deco Brooch | 2005

4 x 4 x ½ inches (10.2 x 10.2 x 1.3 cm)
Seed beads, Czech glass rondelles, pin
back; herringbone stitch with variation,
flat circular herringbone stitch, lacing,
peyote stitch, embellishment

Photo by Melinda Holden

▲ **Alyeska's Jewel** | 2005

Largest, 8 x ½ inches (20.3 x 1.3 cm)
Seed beads, cylinder seed beads,
Swarovski crystals, semiprecious
beads, magnetic clasp, vinyl tubing;
peyote stitch, herringbone stitch,
embellishment
Photo by Melinda Holden

▲ **Granuaile's Crown** | 2003

Necklace, 24 inches (61 cm) long;
pods, 1¼ x ¾ x ½ inches (3.2 x 1.9 x 1.3 cm) each
Seed beads, Czech glass beads, snap; peyote stitch,
herringbone stitch, surface embellishment
Photos by Melinda Holden

" Designing a new piece can be a challenge. Sometimes the design simply jumps out of your brain and your hands know exactly what to do with this information. But then there are times when you think there isn't one more idea left on which to work. When designing for me is 'hot,' I know I'm assured of three new designs from the run of inspiration, and I enjoy every minute of it. When my designing skill is at low tide, I just work on making samples for my workshops. "

◀ **Monet Garden Necklace** │ 1999
24 x 7 x 2 inches (61 x 17.8 x 5.1 cm)
Seed beads, Czech glass beads, triangle beads; peyote stitch, brick stitch, herringbone stitch, fringe, embroidery
Photos by Melinda Holden

Rebecca Brown-Thompson

REFLECTING HER MOVE TO NEW ZEALAND from the United States, the flora and fauna of both countries are given new life in the beadwork of Rebecca Brown-Thompson. Nature in all its forms inspires her. Brown-Thompson is a scientific illustrator by training, but she felt liberated when she first encountered the tactile, dimensional world of beading. She forms pieces—in her mind and in her hands—choosing from an array of stitches, and her versatility distinguishes her work. In *Just Hanging Around*, Brown-Thompson uses right-angle weave, peyote stitch, and bead embroidery to create a delightful neckpiece. She is committed to creating diverse forms, too, including large pectoral necklaces (see *The Guardian*), bracelets (*Shrimp Plant*), belts (*Seascape*), collars (*Pink Collar*), purses (*Huhu Beetle*), and even books (*All Things New Zealand*)—everything is fair game for her beads. Brown-Thompson's work draws the eye because of the large size of many of her fantastic pieces, but it's the exquisite details that viewers will find most inspiring.

▲ **Shrimp Plant** | 2004
7½ x 2 inches (19.5 x 5 cm)
Seed beads; square stitch,
right-angle weave
Photo by Murray Irwin

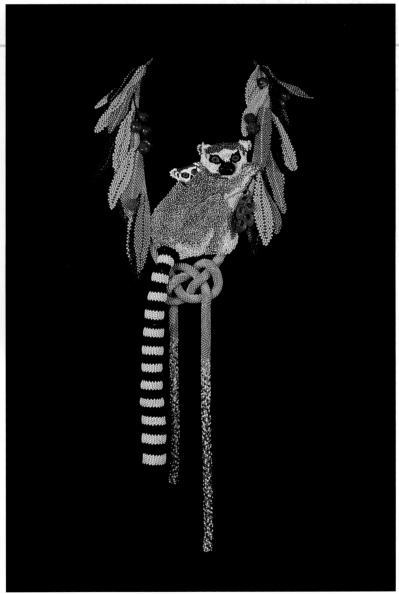

Just Hanging Around | 2001 ▶

24¼ x 7 inches (62 x 18 cm)
Seed beads, plant seeds beads, vintage
glass beads, rope, Fimo polymer clay,
wool padding; bead embroidery, square
stitch, peyote stitch, right-angle weave

Photos by Lloyd Park

" A lot of art today is rushed and conceptual without technique. My desire is to create work that not only has good technique but also the quality and feel of a fine piece of art—something that can be passed down through generations and appreciated for the amount of work that went into making it and the quality of the materials used. I'm jealous of past generations, whose everyday household items were so beautifully crafted that they're still being handed down today. We have precious little of that now. "

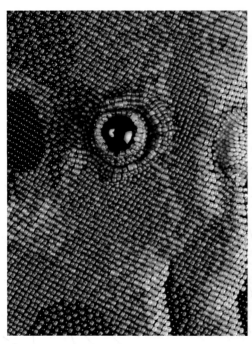

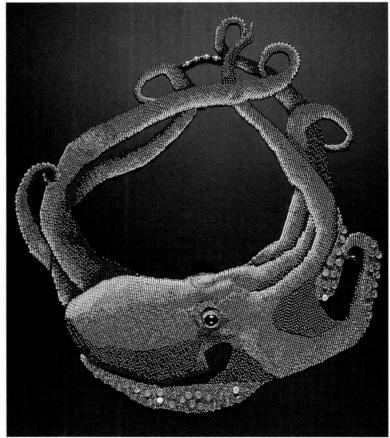

The Guardian | 1999 ▶

18 x 17 inches (46 x 43 cm)
Seed beads, large glass bead;
off-loom square stitch

Photos by Lloyd Park

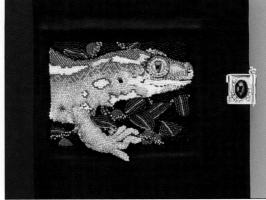

◀ **All Things New Zealand** │ 2004

8½ x 8½ inches (21.5 x 21.5 cm)
Seed beads, snail shell, leather, Ultrasuede,
wool padding, enamel, cardboard, silk
embroidery thread, Fabriano paper, silk
paper, flax paper, glue, glass cabochon,
hand-fabricated sterling silver clasp; bead
embroidery, off-loom peyote stitch, square
stitch, bookbinding techniques

Photos by Murray Irwin

"What influences and inspires me is the natural world. It has been and always will be my primary focus and love affair. Any excuse to be outside—whether to draw, play sports, or camp and tramp—I am there."

▲ Pink Collar | 2005

39¼ x 14⅛ inches (100 x 36 cm)
Seed beads, hand-formed sterling silver, merino wool felt, glue, wood; right-angle weave, square stitch, machine stitching, netting
Photo by artist

▲ Leaf Lei | 2002

13¾ x 7¾ inches (35 x 20 cm)
Seed beads, large glass beads, rope, ceramic button; off-loom right-angle weave, peyote stitch, square stitch, brick stitch, herringbone stitch
Photo by Murray Irwin

▲ **Seascape** | 2004

19⅝ x 2¾ inches (50 x 7 cm)
Seed beads, Ultrasuede, hand-formed copper,
wool padding, Velcro; bead embroidery, peyote
stitch, ruffled peyote stitch, square stitch

Photos by artist

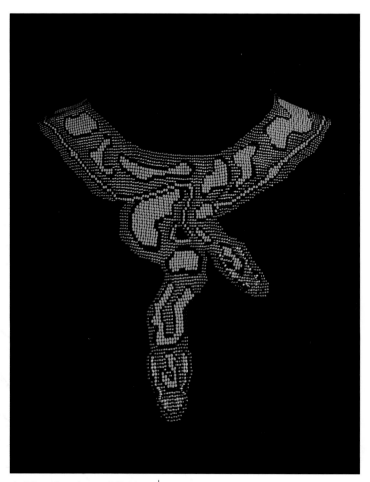

▲ **The Garden of Eden** | 2000

13¾ x 11¾ inches (35 x 30 cm)
Seed beads; off-loom square stitch

Photo by Lloyd Park

▲ **Huhu Beetle** | 2005

9½ x 9½ inches (24 x 24 cm)
Seed beads, merino wool felt, ceramic
button, silk, wool padding; square stitch,
right-angle weave, bead embroidery

Photo by artist

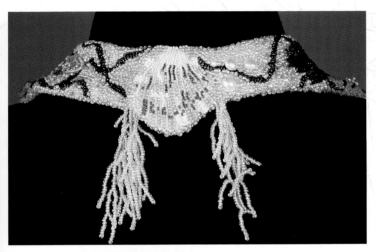

▲ **Portuguese Man-O-War** | 2000

22 x 9 inches (56 x 23 cm)
Seed beads, Swarovski beads, fish bead,
Fimo polymer clay, Ultrasuede; bead
embroidery, peyote stitch, ruffled
peyote stitch, square stitch

Photos by Lloyd Park

" I want the wow factor for
my work. I want people to
enjoy the designs and to be
impressed with what can
be done with beads and
how it was achieved. When
a beaded piece is finished,
there is a huge sense of
accomplishment, especially
after working for more than
200 hours. I can't wait to
see the final piece myself. "

Susan Etcoff Fraerman

THE SHOEMAKER'S LAST is what I immediately envision when I hear the name Susan Etcoff Fraerman. I always knew a story was being told in her work, but for a long time I didn't know the roots of the inspiration: As a teenager, Fraerman spent five post-operative months bound in long leg plaster casts, dreaming of footwear possibilities. Technically, she covers lasts with a smooth layer of beads utilizing stitches like freeform right-angle weave. Then, Fraerman embellishes the surface in select areas to enhance her idea. Her color choices, mostly vintage in appearance, are appropriate both for the stories being told and for the items being covered. *Bound for Glory I* is part of a series in which Fraerman cleansed long-held emotions and claimed her freedom. Fraerman's "shoes" carried her through the death of a family member's baby, with the piece *In Memory of Noah: April 19, 1996–July 13, 1996*, and the death of her father, with *One Soul*. Her beadwork is her catharsis—and our pleasure.

Hannah Banana | 1999 ▶

5½ x 2½ x 3 inches (14 x 6.4 x 7.6 cm)
Glass beads, vintage sugar beads, nylon thread; off-loom beadweaving, right-angle weave, applied beads

Photo by Tom Van Eynde

▲ **Each Child Her Treasure** | 2006

13 x 7 x 10 inches (33 x 17.8 x 25.4 cm)
Seed beads, crystals, 22-karat-gold beads, nylon thread, found object;
off-loom beadweaving, freeform right-angle weave, applied beads
Photo by Tom Van Eynde

" I have a BFA in theater from Boston University, and I yearned to find a creative avenue that would fulfill my need to express myself. One cannot emote alone in the basement. I needed an audience and a cast of characters. I found the answer in narrative beadwork. "

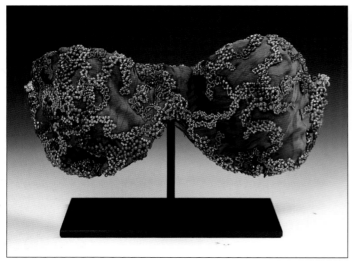 

▲ Bra Book I: "Otherwise" | 2004
   11½ x 8 x 4 inches (29.2 x 20.3 x 10.2 cm)
   Glass beads, metal beads, hand-dyed silk, bridal satin, wire, nylon thread; off-loom
   beadweaving, freeform right-angle weave, bead embroidery, heat transfer
   Photos by Tom Van Eynde

▲ Cassandra | 2007

14 x 10 x 12 inches (35.6 x 25.4 x 30.5 cm)
Seed beads, metal beads, nylon thread, horsehair, found objects;
off-loom beadweaving, freeform right-angle weave, assemblage
Photo by Tom Van Eynde

" I am a storyteller. I weave tales with beads and thread. Often a found object serves as my starting point—the foundation for a metaphor. I work without a predesigned pattern or graph, letting one bead suggest the choice of the next until a rich fabric unfolds. "

▲ **Alteration** | 2002

15 x 9 x 10 inches (38.1 x 22.9 x 25.4 cm)
Seed beads, thermoplastic cotton, pigment, linen, nylon, nylon thread; off-loom beadweaving, freeform right-angle weave, applied beads, thermoplastic manipulation
Photo by Tom Van Eynde

▲ **Bound for Glory I** | 1998

9 x 6½ x 3 inches (22.9 x 16.5 x 7.6 cm)
Seed beads, metal beads, nylon thread, found object;
off-loom beadweaving, right-angle weave

Photos by Tom Van Eynde

" Learning a new stitch does not come easily to me. I spend hours practicing, developing the rhythm of the needle, bead, and thread. Once mastered, the stitches became second nature, allowing me to concentrate on color, line, rhythm, and balance. After a full day of beading, I often fall asleep with the rhythm of the stitch dancing in my head. "

▲ **One Soul** | 2001

9 x 4 x 3½ inches (22.9 x 10.2 x 8.9 cm)
Glass beads, leather, nylon thread, hand-dyed silk organza; off-loom beadweaving, right-angle weave, embellishment, arashi shibori
Photo by Tom Van Eynde

Hecuba | 1996

4½ x 13 x 2 inches (11.4 x 33 x 5.1 cm)
Seed beads, antique metal Austrian button, antique German glass beads, wood, natural fibers, nylon thread, found object; off-loom beadweaving, right-angle weave, applied beads

Photo by Tom Van Eynde

In Memory of Noah: April 19, 1996–July 13, 1996 | 1998

2½ x 4 x 3½ inches (6.4 x 10.2 x 8.9 cm)
Seed beads, metal beads, nylon thread, leather, vinyl; off-loom beadweaving, right-angle weave, applied beads

Photo by Tom Van Eynde

Eleanor Lux

ALL ARTISTS APPROACH their need for expression differently, and most find the element of time essential to the evolution of their work. Eleanor Lux spent 10 years as a stained-glass designer before she took up weaving. She now combines the sensibilities of her two loves in her loom-woven scarves and necklaces. Her studio—a converted old grocery store—holds five floor looms, and one is always being newly threaded so it's ready for beads. In her weavings, Lux plays with texture, light, and transparency. She experiments with pattern in pieces like *Streets of New York* and *Fairy Wings*. *Africa 1940* places large glass rings amidst ripe, bold colors, while pieces like *Dragon Scarf* are much softer in their composition. Much of Lux's work is made in relatively set dimensions, and she boldly explores what's possible within these confines as she continues her distinguished series of beadwork.

Clear Starry Night | 2006 ▶
32 x 1¼ inches (81.3 x 3.2 cm)
Antique seed beads; loom woven
Photo by Cindy Momchilou

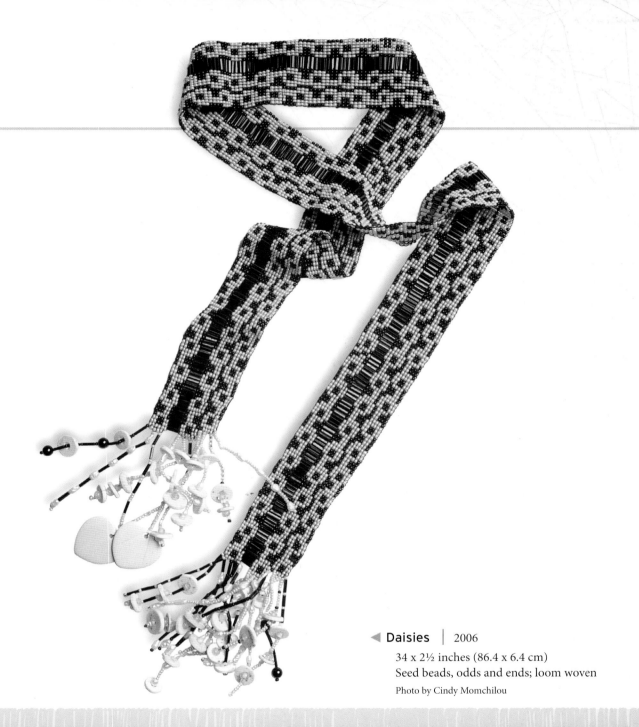

◀ **Daisies** | 2006

34 x 2½ inches (86.4 x 6.4 cm)
Seed beads, odds and ends; loom woven
Photo by Cindy Momchilou

▲ Fairy Wings | 2004

36 x 2 inches (91.4 x 5.1 cm)
Seed beads, Venetian glass beads; loom woven

Photo by Cindy Momchilou

" I love the feel of a piece of beadweaving—the way it drapes across or crunches up in your hand, and the feel of it as you brush it with your fingertips or your cheek. I've learned to give all my beadwork the ability to be handled, because I've found that everyone has difficulty not touching it. I now realize that touching is an important part of enjoying art. "

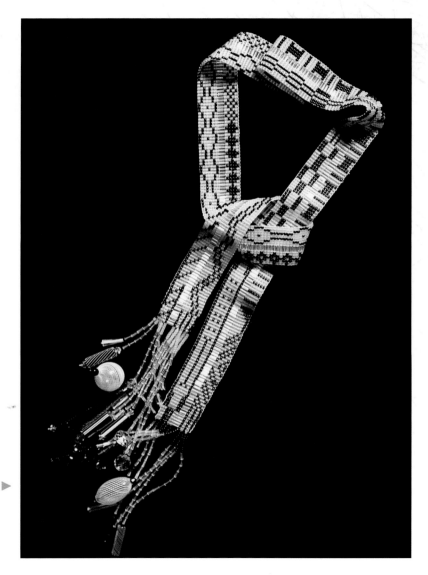

Streets of New York | 2005 ▶

30 x 1½ inches (76.2 x 3.8 cm)
Seed beads, odds and
ends; loom woven

Photo by Cindy Momchilou

" I find in all weaving techniques that design is challenging. It becomes like a game for me. You can't just take a line and let it quickly meander across a piece of paper. It has to meander off one dot at a time. "

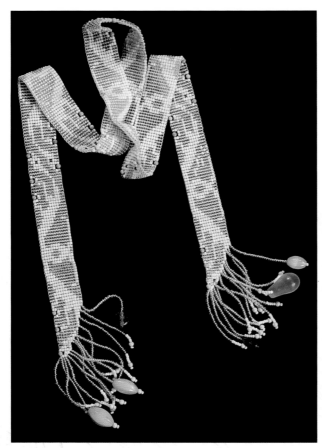

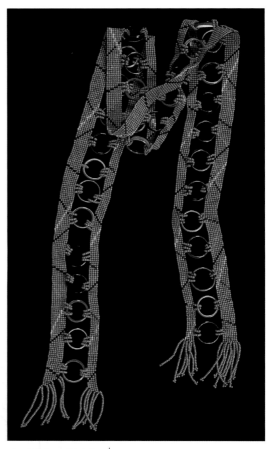

▲ **Dragon Scarf** | 2004
36 x 2 inches (91.4 x 5.1 cm)
Seed beads, turquoise, odds and ends;
loom woven
Photo by Cindy Momchilou

▲ **Africa 1940** | 2000
34 x 3 inches (86.4 x 7.6 cm)
Seed beads, large glass circles;
loom woven
Photo by Cindy Momchilou

◄ **March 15th Electric Storm** | 1996
16 x 7 inches (40.6 x 17.8 cm)
Seed beads; loom woven
Photos by Allen Smith

ELEANOR LUX

" The majority of my artwork is influenced by my feelings about nature, with an emphasis on texture. Beadweaving lends itself to texture like no other medium I know. Another of beadweaving's most treasured specialties is its transparent qualities. Light can pass through certain beads beautifully, and other beads refuse to let light in. I find that adds a great deal of excitement to design possibilities. "

Green Electric Storm | 1995 ▶
16 x 7 inches (40.6 x 17.8 cm)
Seed beads; loom woven
Photo by Allen Smith

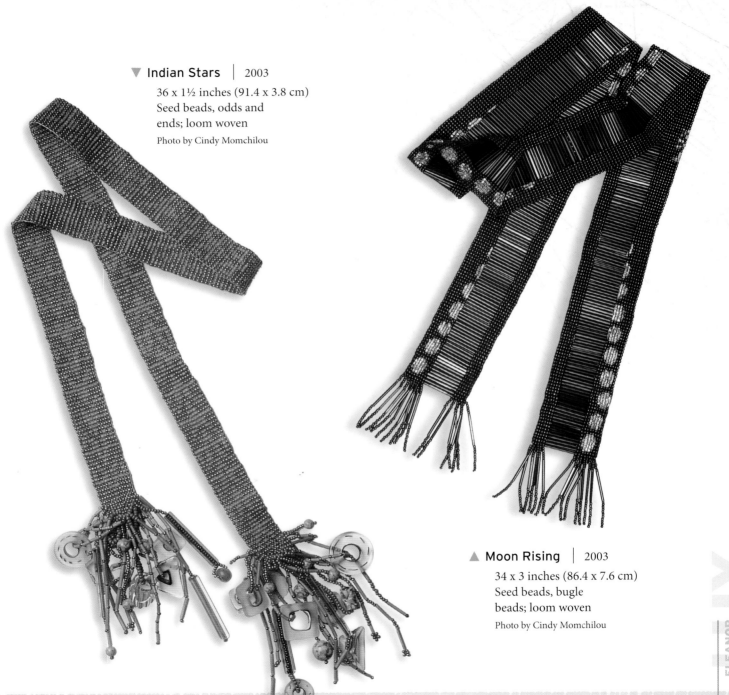

▼ **Indian Stars** | 2003

36 x 1½ inches (91.4 x 3.8 cm)
Seed beads, odds and
ends; loom woven

Photo by Cindy Momchilou

▲ **Moon Rising** | 2003

34 x 3 inches (86.4 x 7.6 cm)
Seed beads, bugle
beads; loom woven

Photo by Cindy Momchilou

Karen Paust

BEING AWARE OF HER PLACE IN THE WORLD, knowing what lives and grows around her, and taking joy and inspiration in all the things nature has to offer is Karen Paust's mode of living and working. Paust's beadwork transports viewers to their own experiences of the natural realm. *Roadside Bouquet* is a botanical wonder, the sort of image we all have come upon, maybe commented on, but then passed quickly because it did not seem grand enough for us. Paust's creations make viewers reconsider such choices.

Paust takes everyday flowers and insects and recreates them in free-form peyote stitch. The amazing realism she achieves in her color gradations are masterful. No detail is overlooked in her work. Each of her flowers is captured, held, and frozen in its own world, waiting for the viewer's sigh. The insects that populate Paust's imagination also receive acknowledgment and tribute: In *Lily and Lacewing* and *Morning Web*, they seem to just be going about business as usual in the midst of a morning dew.

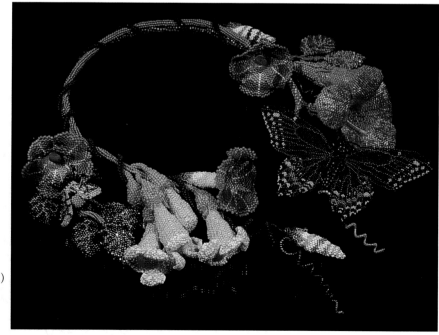

Sunset and Sapphire | 2000 ▶

12 x 10 x 2½ inches (30.5 x 25.4 x 6.4 cm)
Seed beads, copper wire, sterling silver;
peyote stitch, herringbone stitch

Photo by T. E. Crowley

▲ **Vines** │ 1998

11 x 9 x 2 inches (27.9 x 22.9 x 5.1 cm)
Seed beads, copper wire, wood,
sterling silver; peyote stitch

Photo by T. E. Crowley

" Beadwork sprang from my interest in botany. I taught myself how to weave beads together, realizing that beadwork reflected how plant cells connect. Beading allows me to combine sewing, knitting, painting, and sculpting techniques into a very unique art form that interacts with light in a spectacular way. "

▲ **Wildflowers** | 1998

13 x 4 x 2 inches (33 x 10.2 x 5.1 cm)
Seed beads, copper wire; peyote stitch
Photo by T. E. Crowley

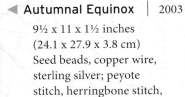 **Autumnal Equinox** | 2003

9½ x 11 x 1½ inches
(24.1 x 27.9 x 3.8 cm)
Seed beads, copper wire,
sterling silver; peyote
stitch, herringbone stitch,
diamond netting

Photo by T. E. Crowley

◀ **Suzen's Hibiscus** | 2002

5 x 5 x 3 inches
(12.7 x 12.7 x 7.6 cm)
Seed beads, copper
wire, sterling silver;
freeform peyote stitch,
diamond netting

Photo by T. E. Crowley

Lily and Lacewing | 1999 ▶

5 x 3½ x 3 inches
(12.7 x 8.9 x 7.6 cm)
Seed beads, copper wire, wood,
sterling silver; freeform peyote
stitch, herringbone stitch

Photo by T. E. Crowley

◀ **Roadside Bouquet** | 2002

11 x 9 x 2 inches
(27.9 x 22.9 x 5.1 cm)
Seed beads, copper wire,
wood, sterling silver; peyote
stitch, herringbone stitch,
right-angle weave, diamond
netting, bead crocheting,
freeform beading

Photo by T. E. Crowley

KAREN **PAUST**

" I have a dead bug collection, but it's not what most people think. It's just a box full of bug body parts. Friends bring me the dead bugs they find, even if it's only half of a bug. I could never kill a butterfly or moth, but if I find one dead I honor its beauty by beading it. I even peel butterflies and moths from my car grill to use as specimens. "

Morning Web | 1997 ▶

10½ x 8½ x 1½ inches
(26.7 x 21.6 x 3.8 cm)
Seed beads, copper wire,
glass teardrops, wood;
peyote stitch

Photo by T. E. Crowley

" The largest shift I've experienced, along with aging, is the awareness of the environmental crisis happening right now. I keep asking myself questions: How can I create work that will inspire people to recycle? What impact does my work have on the environment? "

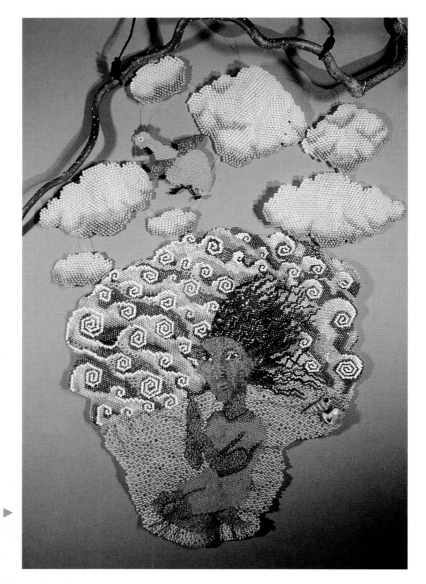

Be Grateful for Where You Are | 1996 ▶

15 x 12 inches (38.1 x 30.5 cm)
Seed beads, branch; freeform peyote stitch
Photo by T. E. Crowley

◀ **Trying to Root** | 1998

26 x 18 x 4 inches
(66 x 45.7 x 10.2 cm)
Seed beads, copper wire;
freeform peyote stitch

Photo by T. E. Crowley

Marcie Stone

PUT SEED BEADS of various sizes, pearls, coral, gemstones, and shells in the hands of Marcie Stone and see what her freeform peyote stitch produces—an organic encrusting of luscious textures. Each of her baskets, necklaces, and sculptures is a seaworthy jewel. Stone does not copy exactly what a reef looks like; rather, she distills the essence of the ocean kingdom. She is a master of judicious color use. *Sunset Neckpiece* and *Oceanic Treasures* are beautiful examples of her color control within the context of improvisational beading. Stone's skills with peyote stitch allow her to build luminous baskets, such as *Apparitions of Linen*, and irresistible shoes, such as *Reef Walker*. Peyote is also the perfect stitch for bezels of irregularly shaped objects, and it is easily increased and decreased, lending itself to Stone's flowing style. Her virtuosity as a beadweaver is secondary in her pieces to her connection to the Earth's oceans—and her insight into the human relationship with them.

▲ **Oceanic Treasures** | 1995
½ x 8½ x 8 inches (1.3 x 21.6 x 20.3 cm)
Seed beads, coral beads, shells, turquoise beads, glass beads; sculptural peyote stitch
Photo by Melinda Holden

▲ **Sunset Neckpiece** | 2007

½ x 7½ x 7½ inches (1.3 x 19.1 x 19.1 cm)
Seed beads, glass cabochons by Greg
Hanson, amber beads, turquoise beads,
glass beads; sculptural peyote stitch
Photo by Greg Hanson

½ x 8 x 8 inches (1.3 x 20.3 x 20.3 cm)
Seed beads, tourmaline beads, glass
beads, pearls, glass cabochons by
Greg Hanson, abalone pieces;
sculptural peyote stitch
Photo by Greg Hanson

" I start a piece by picking a focal point that
intrigues me. Then, I lay out a selection of
beads like a painter's palette. From this palette I make
spontaneous choices that evolve into a biomorphic synthesis of textures
and colors. I love the way the textures of the beads play against each other,
creating jeweled encrustations influenced by primitive art and organic forms. "

MARCIE STONE

◀ **Boulder Opal Necklace** | 2005

½ x 7¼ x 7¼ inches (1.3 x 18.4 x 18.4 cm)
Seed beads, Boulder opal beads, pearls, opal
chips, glass beads; sculptural peyote stitch

Photos by Greg Hanson

Subterranean Landscape | 1998 ▶

10½ x 24 x 3 inches (26.7 x 61 x 7.6 cm)
Seed beads, coral beads, garnets, shells,
antique glass, wire, batting, soft sculpture
armature; sculptural peyote stitch

Photos by Melinda Holden

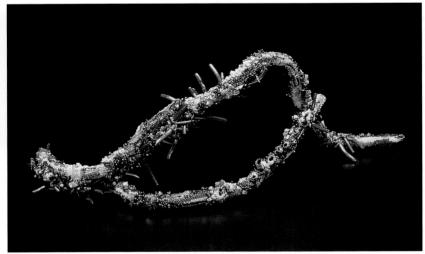

" When I start a piece, I'm not interested in knowing exactly what it's going to look like when it's finished. I find it way more exciting to watch it take shape under my fingertips. This leaves the piece open to many unexpected surprises. I really am interested in organic forms, and I think of my pieces growing, to some extent, by themselves. "

▲ **Nedra's Wedding Neckpiece** | 2001
½ x 8 x 8 inches (1.3 x 20.3 x 20.3 cm)
Seed beads, mobe pearl, pearls, opal chips, labradorite, smoky quartz, antique beads, modern beads; sculptural peyote stitch
Photo by Fred Salamon

Reef Walker | 2000 ▶

6⅞ x 4½ x 9½ inches (17.4 x 11.4 x 24.1 cm)
Seed beads, coral beads, turquoise beads, glass
beads, Varaform; sculptural peyote stitch

Photos by Melinda Holden

◀ **Coral Reef** │ 1994

7 x 5 x 5 inches (17.8 x 12.7 x 12.7 cm)
Seed beads, turquoise beads, coral beads, shells, silk,
pine needles; coiled basketry, sculptural peyote stitch
Photos by Melinda Holden

" Peyote stitch has always been my technique of choice. I find it totally user-friendly, allowing my pieces

to grow in spontaneous manners. This stitch is pleased to grow in any direction I choose to push it in.

When varying the size of beads I'm using, it creates wonderful sculptural formations. "

Apparitions of Linen | 1997

3 x 2½ x 2½ inches (7.6 x 6.4 x 6.4 cm)
Seed beads, coral beads, pearls,
amber beads; sculptural peyote stitch
Photo by Melinda Holden

La Chaussure du Mouchette | 2003 ▶

6½ x 3½ x 9½ inches (16.5 x 8.9 x 24.1 cm)
Seed beads, glass beads, sequins, Varaform,
silk ribbon; sculptural peyote stitch
Photo by Melinda Holden

MARCIE STONE

LOVETT

Dallas Lovett

MIXING WIRE AND BEADS COMES NATURALLY to Dallas Lovett, and his sense of design utilizes these materials to maximum advantage. Glass seed beads, pearls, and lampworked beads blend with sterling silver wire to create woven wonders for body adornment. Lovett's work has an imaginative flow and movement generated by the techniques of wire weaving and wrapping he uses and the shapes he designs. His *Flight and Fantasy Necklace* demonstrates how a static medium can be made fluid: Half-moon shapes laced with beads serpentine around the neck, caught at the narrows with coils and pearls. Lovett explores texture in his work, sometimes by increasing or decreasing a tube's diameter or by adding keshi pearls and other beads—*Keshi Bracelet* and *Sand and Sable Bracelet* are excellent examples. Clean lines, attention to fine detail, and inventive design help make Lovett's work modern, sophisticated, and in high demand.

Sand and Sable Bracelet | 2005 ▶

7½ x ¾ inches (19.1 x 1.9 cm)
Seed beads, Bali silver, keshi pearls,
lampworked beads, sterling silver
wire; wire weaving
Photo by Robert Diamonte

▲ **Flight and Fantasy Necklace** | 2005

18 x 7 x 4 inches (45.7 x 17.8 x 10.2 cm)
Seed beads, freshwater pearls,
sterling silver wire; wire weaving
Photo by Robert Diamonte

▲ Boyer Wave | 2003

3¾ x ⅝ inches (9.5 x 1.5 cm)
Seed beads, diachronic glass, Bali silver, sterling
silver wire; wire weaving and fabrication

Photo by Robert Diamonte

" The desire to create a new design is what drives me artistically. It obsesses my every waking moment until I have it worked out in my head, at which time I put it on paper. I start with a shape, which leads me to the design of the piece. I begin to incorporate the desired textures, smooth or twisted wire, seed beads or pearls, and symmetrical or asymmetrical shapes. All of this leads to the final engineering of the piece of jewelry and what it will become. "

▲ Pod | 2005

2½ x ¾ inches (6.4 x 1.9 cm)
Seed beads, pearls, lampworked bead,
Bali silver, sterling silver wire; wire weaving
Photo by Robert Diamonte

" As a native of the southwest United States, I am very inspired by the rich textures and brilliant colors of the many regions of the Sonoran Desert; the red rocks of Sedona, Arizona; and the majestic form of the Grand Canyon. The design and shape of many pieces of my work reflect this regional influence. "

───────────────

▲ **Grecian Bracelet** | 2004
  3½ x ¾ inches (8.9 x 1.9 cm)
  Seed beads, freshwater pearls,
  sterling silver wire; wire weaving

  Photo by Robert Diamonte

▲ **Enchanted Bracelet** | 2006
  7½ x ½ inches (19.1 x 1.3 cm)
  Seed beads, pearls, sterling
  silver wire; wire weaving

  Photo by Robert Diamonte

◀ **Desire Necklace** | 2003

21 x 1½ inches (53.3 x 3.8 cm)
Seed beads, keshi pearls, Bali silver,
lampworked beads, sterling silver
wire; wire weaving

Photo by Robert Diamonte

▲ **Keshi Bracelet** | 2002

7½ x ¾ inches (19.1 x 1.9 cm)
Seed beads, keshi pearls,
potato pearls, sterling silver
wire; wire wrapping

Photo by Robert Diamonte

▲ **Galaxy Necklace** | 2005

22 x 3 x ¾ inches (55.9 x 7.6 x 1.9 cm)
Seed beads, freshwater pearls, lampworked beads,
Bali silver, sterling silver wire; wire weaving

Photos by Robert Diamonte

" The journey of an artist can be slow. It is dedication and diligence in practicing your art form that eventually defines you and your work. Even when you constantly weave and design, time still will hone your skills and refine your technique. "

◀ **Ornate Treasures** │ 2002
4½ x 2½ inches (11.4 x 6.4 cm)
Seed beads, pearls, Swarovski crystals, lampworked bead, sterling silver wire, wire weaving
Photo by Robert Diamonte

Margo C. Field

LIGHT, AIRY, AND REPLETE WITH warm floral chintz, the beadwork of Margo C. Field features many varieties of flowers and leaves, which take shape to create necklaces and other forms of exquisite beauty. Field has a way of choosing the right technique—peyote, herringbone, right-angle weave—to make the flowers and leaves come alive. And if there isn't a known stitch that will provide the results she seeks, she steps out of the box and makes up her own.

Field employs a softness of color in her palette that is soothing and engaging. Her visual textures enliven the work, and a sense of movement and dimension lighten the mood in her accessible pieces. Her jewelry turns the entire garden into wearable art. Field also demonstrates her sense of play in the non-jewelry pieces *Agnes & Irma* and *"Miss Kitty I Love You."* These pieces demonstrate the boundless talents of this beadweaving innovator and fine artist.

Flowers for Helene | 2002 ▶

8 x 4 x 6 inches (20.3 x 10.2 x 15.2 cm)
Seed beads, wire, cactus wood;
peyote stitch, herringbone
stitch, invented stitches
Photo by Pat Berrett

Pentafoil Flowers | 2002 ▶

12 x 8 x 1 inches (30.5 x 20.3 x 2.5 cm)
Seed beads, glass beads, freshwater
pearls; netting, invented stitches
Photo by Pat Berrett

" Because of my math and chemistry education, a lot of my creations are based on mathematics and geometry. I love intricacy based on geometric form. However, because of my superstitious nature, I avoid certain numbers and often use my favorite numbers. So, I make decisions based on both logic and faith. "

Floral Cascade | 1997 ▶

12 x 7 x 1¼ inches (30.5 x 17.8 x 3.2 cm)
Seed beads, glass beads; peyote
stitch, invented stitches

Photo by Pat Berrett

MARGO C. FIELD

◀ **Leaf Motif Opus Three** | 2002
13 x 9 x ½ inches (33 x 22.9 x 1.3 cm)
Seed beads, glass beads; netting
Photo by Pat Berrett

" I'm most comfortable working with the colors found in nature. I'm in love with the natural greens and yellows that show new growth and the greens and blues that show cool forest shadows. Some of my designs have more then 10 colors of green. I'm always excited to find a new color, because it may lead to a flow of inspiration. "

◄ **Bakelite & Trumpet Vines** │ 2000
12 x 7 x 1 inches (30.5 x 17.8 x 2.5 cm)
Seed beads, Bakelite pieces; peyote stitch,
branched fringe, invented stitches
Photo by Pat Berrett

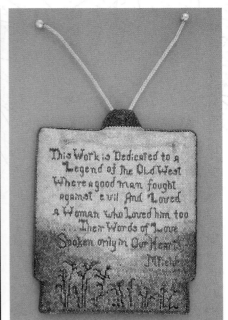

◄ **"Miss Kitty I Love You"** | 1998

12½ x 6½ x ¼ inches (31.8 x 16.5 x 0.6 cm)
Seed beads, fabric, wire, crystals;
appliqué, peyote stitch

Photos by Pat Berrett

Agnes & Irma | 2004 ▶

9½ x 5 x 5 inches (24.1 x 12.7 x 12.7 cm)
Seed beads, glass beads, wire, wood; appliqué,
peyote stitch, netting, right-angle weave

Photo by Pat Berrett

" Most of my early memories
are of the flowers in my
mother's garden. My main
inspirations come from nature,
and from flowers and leaves
in particular. When I was
five, my mother acquired a
book on how to make real-
looking flowers from crepe
paper. I made all the flowers
throughout my childhood. I
still have the book. "

◀ **Margo's Rita Ville** │ 2007
   9 x 6 x ¾ inches (22.9 x 15.2 x 1.9 cm)
   Seed beads, margarita crystals,
   glass pearls; herringbone stitch,
   netting, branched fringe
   Photo by Pat Berrett

Virginia L. Blakelock

THE BLENDING OF DOTS OF COLORS to achieve an elaborate image in her mind's eye shows Virginia L. Blakelock's training as a painter. In her execution, every detail is considered—there's no rushing a piece by Blakelock. Each bead is checked for size and shape, with careful thought given to how the color of one bead mixes visually with another, and how a finished wearable piece will lay on the body. *Daphnis nerii (Oleander Hawk Moth)* is an outstanding example of color blends created with 494 seed beads used per square inch (6.5 square centimeters). From under the ground, as seen in *Crude Root*, to the height of the heavens in *Galaxy NGC1300*, Blakelock evokes the power of nature as it relates to the human experience and our world. The back section of *Nagasaki* appears to be photographed poorly, as if flooded by a flash; actually, the light area is woven into the piece. Blakelock's spectacular, ambitious work never fails to surprise the eye, even as it delights viewers.

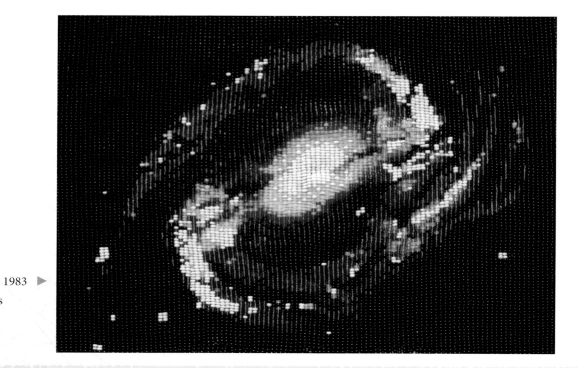

Galaxy NGC1300 | 1983 ▶
12¼ x 12¾ x ¹⁄₁₆ inches
(31.1 x 32.3 x 0.1 cm)
Seed beads; loomwork
Photo by Gary Lee Betts

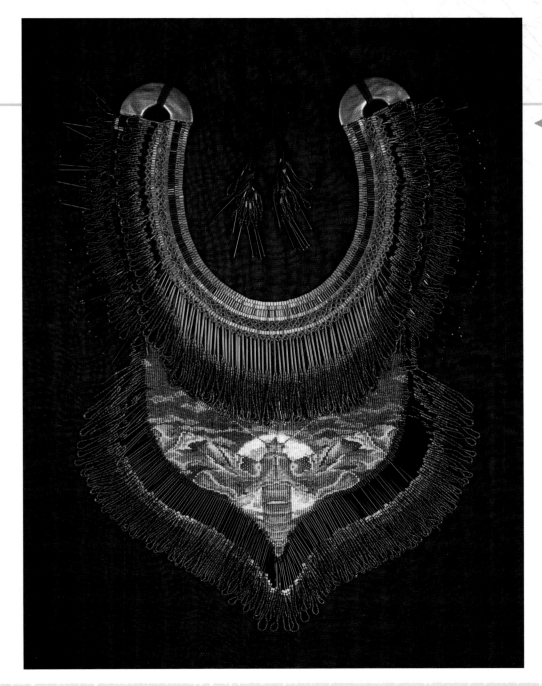

◀ **Daphnis nerii
(Oleander Hawk Moth)** | 1984–1985

16 x 9 x ³⁄₁₆ inches (40.6 x 22.8 x .48 cm)
Seed beads, bugle beads; loomwork,
ladder stitch, netting, looped fringes

Photo by Gary Lee Betts

Calligraphy Beetles | 1988–1999 ▶

25 x 15 x 2 inches (63.5 x 38.1 x 5 cm)
Seed beads, bugle beads, bone skulls,
pressed glass drops; loomwork,
ladder stitch, netting

Photo by Gary Lee Betts

" As a teenager, I lived for four years
in Karachi, Pakistan, so Islamic
calligraphy and Hindi art were
important design influences for me.
My inspiration comes from nature.
I look to it for colors, textures,
patterns, light, and mood. Some
of my most important pieces were
made during the 10 years I lived in a
190-square-foot (17.6 square meter)
cabin in the woods and did concrete
work with my husband. **"**

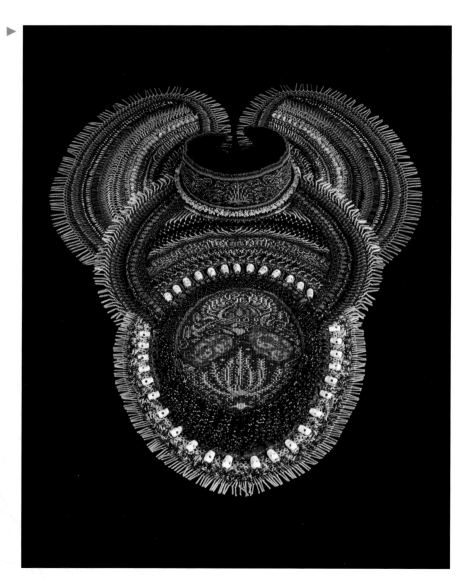

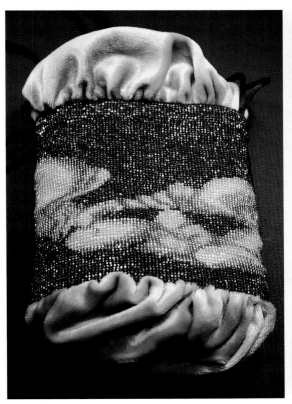
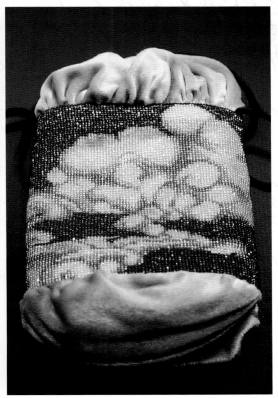

▲ **Cloud Purse** | 1978

8¼ x 4¾ x 2 inches (20.9 x 12 x 5 cm)
Triple-cut Czech seed beads,
panne velvet; loomwork

Photos by artist

▲ **Trilobite** | 1998–2004

9½ x 4½ x 1 inches (24.1 x 11.4 x 2.5 cm)
Cylinder seed beads, triple-cut Czech beads,
seed beads; flat peyote stitch, brick stitch,
flat herringbone stitch, shibori pleated silk

Photo by Gary Lee Betts

Empress | 1984 ▶

16 x 9 x 2 inches (40.6 x 22.8 x 5 cm)
Triple-cut Czech seed beads,
leather; loomwork

Photo by Gary Lee Betts

" In early pieces, few beads were available, so I could only work with design. Once, in the early days, I drove to Blackfoot, Idaho, and bought $800 worth of beads. My husband, Gary, later confessed he thought I'd lost my mind. But, incredibly, he continued to encourage me. After 20 years of bead collecting, I can now play with subtle colors and transitions. "

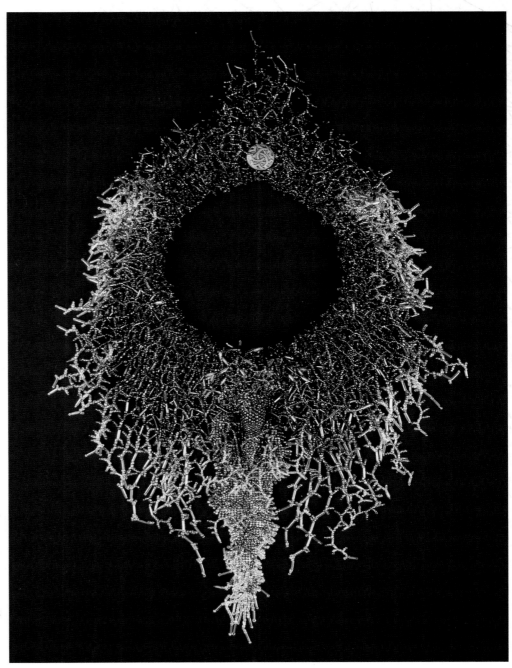

Crude Root | 1988 ▶

16 x 8 x 1 inches (40.6 x 20.3 x 2.5 cm)
Triple-cut Czech seed beads, bugle beads; loomwork, ladder stitch, tubular peyote stitch, kinky fringe
Photo by Gary Lee Betts

First Night | 2000–2006 ▶

14 x 7½ x ¾ inches (35.5 x19 x 1.9 cm)
Seed beads, Czech pressed glass beads;
flat peyote stitch, netting, shaped fringes
Photo by Gary Lee Betts

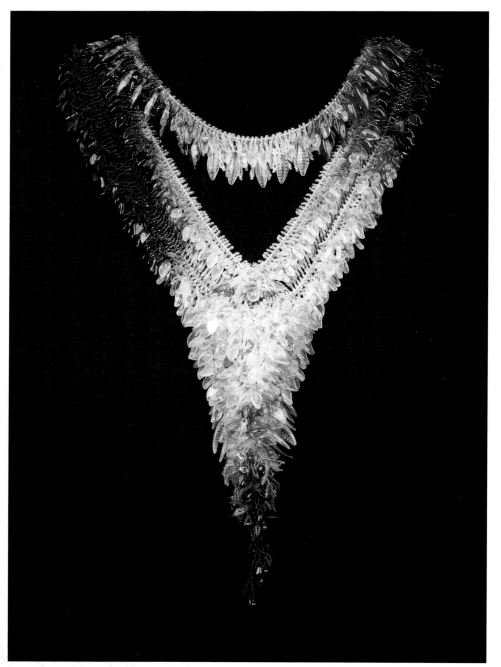

" I'm still learning about bead art. Every piece investigates technique and experiments with color. Awareness is all. Once a piece is started, I try to have a dialogue with it. I always hope for the unexpected. I want the piece to surprise me. I'm never sure of the unconscious motives behind my work. "

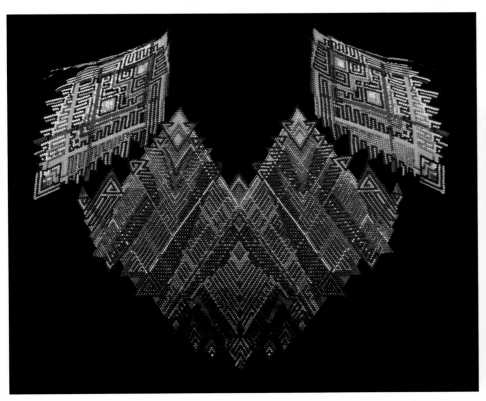

▲ **Nagasaki** | 2000–2006

18½ x 16 x ¹⁄₁₆ inches (46.9 x 40.6 x 0.1 cm)
Cylinder seed beads, triple-cut Czech seed beads; brick stitch
Photos by Gary Lee Betts

Jo Ann Baumann

JUST AS BEADWEAVING and beads are essential parts of Jo Ann Baumann's life, so, too, is her life essential to her beadwork. In it, the joys and trials of her life find themselves retold and reborn. A woman clearly aware of and engaged by life's hills and valleys, Baumann uses her beadweaving to express her perspectives on the journey. *Woman with Attitude* captures the sassiness of a woman over 50, harboring a "do not mess with me" outlook that still keeps a sense of humor about aging. Indeed, humor is prevalent throughout Baumann's work—less reflected in the subjects she addresses than in her takes on them and her uses of color. *Menopausal Mama aka All Strung Out* is bright and cheerful, hiding the fact that as you advance through life the changes sometimes can be a bit overwhelming and gray. Baumann's *Carnival* necklace of beaded beads and earrings are just happy, likely to induce smiles on even the cloudiest day. Joyous combinations of colors take viewers along with Baumann to Mexico, the sea, and memories of her grandmother's garden in her unforgettable work.

▲ **Menopausal Mama aka All Strung Out** │ 1997
22 x 10 x 9 inches (55.9 x 25.4 x 22.9 cm)
Seed beads, telephone wire, thread spools,
silk fabric strips; brick stitch
Photos by Tom Van Eynde

▲ **Woman with Attitude** | 1997

4 x 7 x 2 inches (10.2 x 17.8 x 5.1 cm)
Seed beads, triangles, crystals, lampworked beads, braided bead strap;
right-angle weave, two- and three-drop peyote stitch

Photo by Larry Sanders

" My life always has been about creativity. When I am not beading, I am making up recipes, putting a weird outfit together, or thinking up a different way to execute a project. If I live to be 500, I still will never have enough time to act on all my ideas. My work reflects my personal journey and my continual search to find and redefine myself. I'm grateful that I'm free to create every day. "

Broken | 2005 ▶

10 x 7 x 7 inches (25.4 x 17.8 x 17.8 cm)
Seed beads, hand-dyed silk organza,
thread spools, concrete base; brick
stitch, right-angle weave fringe
Photo by Guy Nicol

Memories of Mexico | 1999 ▼

5 x 5 x 2½ inches (12.7 x 12.7 x 6.4 cm)
Seed beads, antique sequins, flower
beads, squares, fabric, polyester
fiberfill stuffing; embroidery,
peyote ruffling, fringe

Photos by Tom Van Eynde

▲ **Sea Spirit Series** | 1996–1999

4 x 4 x 4 inches (10.2 x 10.2 x 10.2 cm)
Seed beads, flower beads; right-angle weave,
peyote ruffling, herringbone stitch, fringe

Photos by Tom Van Eynde

" In using beads as an expressive art form, one idea seems to evolve from another. I get an idea and sketch it, and sometimes, to my surprise, the finished piece actually looks like the sketch. Often as I'm working I ask myself 'How far can I take this?' My work seems to take on a life of its own. "

◀ Happy | 2003
14 x 14 x 1½ inches (35.6 x 35.6 x 3.8 cm)
Seed beads, wooden beads, lampworked beads; right-angle weave
Photo by Larry Sanders

7 x 4 x 1½ inches (17.8 x 10.2 x 3.8 cm)
Seed beads, crystals, Ultrasuede,
interfacing, vintage kimono fabric,
metal closure; bead embroidered,
peyote stitch, right-angle weave

Photos by Larry Sanders

◀ **Carnival** | 2002

14 x 14 x 1½ inches (35.6 x 35.6 x 3.8 cm)
Seed beads, triangle beads, teardrops,
wooden beads, lampworked spacers;
right-angle weave

Photo by Larry Sanders

JO ANN BAUMANN

" My creative passion has led
me to a place deep within
myself where my inspiration
and visions are expressed by
the magic seductiveness of
beading. My spiritual journey
begins with an idea, a needle
and thread, and delicious
piles of colorful beads. "

Flowers on the Vine | 2002–2003 ▶
15 x 10 x 2 inches (38.1 x 25.4 x 5.1 cm)
Seed beads, cylinder beads, wired plastic
tubing; right-angle weave, peyote stitch
Photo by Larry Sanders

About the Curator

CAROL WILCOX WELLS is a renowned beadweaving artist and teacher. She is the author  of *Creative Bead Weaving: A Contemporary Guide to Classic Off-Loom Stitches* and *The Art & Elegance of Beadweaving: New Jewelry Designs with Classic Stitches*, both from Lark Books. Her work has been exhibited internationally and featured in *Ornament, Lapidary Journal, Bead & Button,* and *Beadwork* magazines. Carol teaches beginning and advanced beadweaving techniques, and she has created numerous beadwork kits. She lives in Asheville, North Carolina.

Carol writes:

"Beadweaving is in my blood—it took a long time to find me, but when it did it wove itself deep within my very soul. I can't imagine a day without beads or thoughts of what I can do with them. The 1972 book *How to Do Bead Work* by Mary White was my first beading book, and with it I taught myself how to bead on a loom. When *Ornament* magazine featured the loom work of Virginia Blakelock, I knew that I had to take a class with her, and I did in 1991 at the Penland School of Crafts in Penland, North Carolina. I was introduced to the off-loom beadweaving techniques she describes in her 1990 book *Those Bad Bad Beads*, and my life changed.

"As I played with peyote stitch and learned its idiosyncrasies, I began making amulet bags and wearing them to meetings of the Bead Society of Greater Chicago. Other members asked me to teach them the stitch. One thing led to another, and soon I was teaching all over the Chicago area, before I moved back to Asheville, North Carolina, in 1993.

"Living in Asheville gave me the opportunity to become a member of the Southern Highland Craft Guild. At the new member show, Carol Taylor, an editor at Lark Books, saw my work. She asked if I would write a book about off-loom beadweaving techniques. I said yes, and my life changed again. *Creative Bead Weaving* was published in 1996. My life was filled with teaching, beading, and running a mail-order beading supply business. In 2002, I published another Lark Books title, *The Art & Elegance of Beadweaving.* I continue to do and teach what I love—off-loom beadweaving techniques."

Learn more about Carol's work at www.schoolofbeadwork.com.

Portrait Photographers

Thank you to the photographers whose portraits of the beadweaving artists appear in this book:

Jeanette Ahlgren, photo by Duane Bibby
Jo Ann Baumann, photo by Larry Baumann
Virginia L. Blakelock, photo by Gary Lee Betts
Rebecca Brown-Thompson, photo by Robert Thompson
Sonya Clark, photo by Tom McInvaille
Marcia DeCoster, photo by Mark DeCoster
Rev. Wendy Ellsworth, photo by David Ellsworth
Margo C. Field, photo by Pat Berrett
Linda Fifield, photo by Jack Fifield
Diane Fitzgerald, photo by Michael Malloy
Leslie Frazier, photo by Tom Frazier
NanC Meinhardt, photo by Harriet Kohn
Rachel Nelson-Smith, photo by Linda Hixon
Huib Petersen, photo by Susan Strolis
Melanie Potter, photo by Scott Potter
Cynthia Rutledge, photo by Melinda Holden
Joyce J. Scott, photo by John Dean
Sherry Serafini, photo by Tim Luxbacher
Natasha St. Michael, photo by Garfield
Marcie Stone, photo by Christopher Perez
Carol Wilcox Wells, photo by Scott Potter
Laura Willits, photo by Philip Arny
Amolia Willowsong, photo by Tim Barnwell

The photos of David K. Chatt, Sharon M. Donovan, Susan Etcoff Fraerman, Valerie Hector, Laura Leonard, Dallas Lovett, Eleanor Lux, Laura McCabe, Maggie Meister, Ann Tevepaugh Mitchell, Karen Paust, Don Pierce, Madelyn C. Ricks, and Sharmini Wirasekara are self-portraits.

Acknowledgments

Carol Wilcox Wells, curator of this collection, offered terrific insight and intelligence in selecting the beadweaving pieces and writing introductions for each master artist. I both deeply respect her expertise and enthusiasm about this versatile art form and appreciate the good humor and integrity with which she approached the curating process.

My heartfelt thanks go to the beadweavers who submitted exciting and innovative work for the book. The artists' thoughtful and sometimes funny and provocative commentary illuminates their processes and personalities, even as their magnificent creative efforts shine brightly.

The contributions of the Lark Books staff to bring all this work together in such a beautiful way were considerable. Julie Hale's stellar editorial eye and sensibility strengthened the book immeasurably, and we received able assistance in editorial matters from Cassie Moore, Dawn Dillingham, Rosemary Kast, and Jeffrey Japp. Dana Irwin brought wise, strong vision to her art direction, executing a terrific series design by Kristi Pfeffer. The art-production team of Jeff Hamilton, Shannon Yokeley, Craig Shapley, and Eva Reitzel supported Dana diligently.

— Ray Hemachandra, Senior Editor

Index of Featured Artists